Your Story, Our Story

Intentionally Dating on Purpose

By Tyler Grady Moore

To my Peyton "Mia" Moore

Intentional

Purposeful

Always with the Father's approval

I wrote this book for the singles, for the dating, for those who might be in a three year relationship but never actually made it official. I wrote this book and devotional for the countless people totally turned around when it comes to dating *today*. I wrote this book and devotional for those with a failed marriage and they're wondering if this is the end of the story. I wrote this book and devotional for people like you and me. There are scriptures to focus on during each chapter, some are short verses, some are whole stories. We have devotional questions just for you as an individual, and we have devotional questions for you to do together. Those are called *Couples Devotional*. And last but not least there is an *Application* for you to do together that week, or day. These questions and applications begin in Chapter 1.

If you wanted a devotional to go through as a couple and specifically improve your relationship immediately, Section 2 and 3 are specifically for you. For everyone else, start at the beginning. You'll get the context of our story and some devotional questions just for you as well. This is the time before me and my wife were together and I know it can apply to your life also. If you are looking to utilize this book primarily as a devotional for your relationship, we would recommend doing one chapter a week, then meet up and discuss the content and questions in person.

Peyton and I did several devotionals before we got married. And I did a *ton* of reading when it comes to relationships and marriage to try to prepare for getting hitched. So I pray this book and devotional will bless you like Peyton and I were blessed.

Also, if you're new to this whole Jesus thing, or maybe you don't really know what you believe, but you desperately want some help when it comes to this dating thing. I would recommend reading Chapter 4, the Section 2 Overview, and Chapters 9, 10 and 12, along with Chapters 15 and 19. I think these will be the most user-friendly for you no matter where you're at in your faith journey. Thank you so much again for considering this book, even if you're not sure what to consider about this whole Jesus guy. He's for you and not against you.

Table of Contents

An Introduction

When I started following Jesus, actually following him by having a relationship with him and not just another religion; I knew I had to take a break from the dating scene and detox from all the damage secular dating had on my life, emotions, mental-health and soul.

It may be considered *secular* dating to Christians but to everyone else it's just dating. You know, a sporadic encounter or two peaking interest in one another, sparking a physical attraction. It's an exchange of words, an exchange of contact info. A little bit of fun, a little bit of messing around. And the next thing you know, you've been in this *thing* or relationship for years now. A thing you need to fulfill your deep desires of affection and acceptance.

You've been in this thing years now, but you have no idea how you got here or where it's going. You call each other boyfriend and girlfriend, but you never actually talked about it seriously before or remember being asked. You live together, maybe have kids together or possibly got a place together. Although you need it, it's a *thing* that permeates low-grade disappointment continuously in your life. Then, soon enough, it ends in major disappointment. Check the research sociologists have done on cohabitating.

If this is what secular dating entails, why is it that dating other believers follows suit? Why does dating other people who believe in Jesus feel just as complicated, just as confusing, just as chaotic? Is it really the lack of sex? Or is it the abundance of temptation to have sex which hinders the life *abundant* Jesus was referring to here and now?

I know I can speak for all of the prodigals out there when it comes to the radical difference of trying to date in a Christ-honoring way. It's a complete one-eighty to the way we used to do things. But what about the girls like my wife? She knew plenty of Christian boys growing up, but none of them were ever brave enough to ask her out, let alone to prom; in fear of being rejected by the hot chick in group. Girls, are you really supposed to let passive boys float from the friend-zone into your boyfriend without the courage of ever being *intentional* about how they feel towards you? Or will you continue to have to make the first move? Is that really the type of man you want anyways? Or are they just the ones you settle for?

Or what about guys like my brother? Guys that would accidentally entice every desperate Christian girl in the ministry to join the intern team he's on. Hoping, praying, and stalking that he's the answer to their deep-seeded insecurities they haven't surrendered to Jesus. Is there something more fulfilling than just saying yes to the next girl who's crazy for a ring by spring semester?

A little harsh, I know. But more and more these stories become all too true. Passive men not fighting for the one they like and insecure girls trying to fill those wounds with a relationship. I don't know what to say. I end up having more questions for my friends than when they come to me for answers. And when it comes to having all of the answers, I don't. But after twenty plus coffee dates in twenty-four months of waiting, and the painstaking process of God purging out *my will* from what I thought was best. I knew there was a way to pursue the right one and date her that was rooted in the Bible, rooted in the promises of scripture, and rooted in Jesus Christ. I knew there was a way to date in which "God causes everything to work together for the good of those who love God and are called according to his purpose for them," (Romans 8:28). And from this truth I learned the way to date involved being intentional, purposeful, and always having the Father's approval.

This is my story, my wife's story. This is your story.

Section 1 Overview

The Father's Approval

[2] Do not be conformed to this world, but be transformed by the renewal of your mind, that by testing you may discern what is the will of God, what is good and acceptable and perfect.
- Romans 12:2

The will of God has always been a confusing thing for me growing up. Growing up in a Christian home, my mom dragged me and my brother to church every weekend. I liked my church as a kid. I even enjoyed the messages our pastor would speak. I still love them today. But when it came to this whole God thing, you know, the he's God and I'm obviously *not* thing; I spent most of my time trying to be good so I wouldn't go to hell. I did what I enjoyed growing up, playing sports and chasing girls. And by the time college came around, I became pretty good at both. I went from one relationship to the next. Honestly hoping they would work out. But they never did. It went from one bad blow up to the next. And I never understood what God was doing. I never understood God's will in letting them fall apart.

I was obviously a good guy, and they we're seemingly good girls. It seemed like the math was lined up to equal a good relationship. But they didn't. And when it came to God's will for my dating life, I didn't know what it was. And how could I? I never read my Bible, I never searched for the answers to the questions I had, and I never sought advice from Godly men or women more experienced than me in faith. I just did my thing throughout the week and let God do his. And once a week for an hour we'd convene at church, I'd layout my sins, pray for forgiveness and go on my merry way.

I never knew God had a *will* for my dating life. I never knew God actually had a purpose for it. I never knew God even really cared about who I was seeing, or who I was interested in. I thought everyone had a destiny woven together by some bearded guy in the sky according to what he wanted. I never knew there was a personal God, who delighted in his children's joy. I never knew he was *like* a father, not just *called* a father, rejoicing at giving his kids good gifts. It wasn't until life shipwrecked me on the rocks of broken dreams and dead relationships that I was willing to listen. It wasn't until I had received and lost everything I ever chased that I was willing to sit down with someone closer to God than me and hear God's two-cents on what he wills for my life to be like. It wasn't until I came back to the Father, barely able to get to my knees and beg forgiveness for the prodigal waste I've been that I felt the sweet embracing tears of mercy and grace. The nail scarred hands that grabbed me so tight and would never let me go. And the love of a Heavenly Father who would give everything for me, knowing I'd spit in his face; only to welcome me back home with a celebration and a feast.

I never knew it was a relationship. I never knew he loved me with a love that would conquer sin and death. I never knew I could know him intimately through Jesus Christ. How could I have known how good and perfect and more than acceptable his will for my life could be! Impossible! It's too good to be true. I guess that's why it's called the *good news*, because we can. And just like the apostle Paul, someone who was conformed to the world of Jewish legalism and was later transformed in Jesus Christ, we too can be transformed, and not just our Sunday morning agendas either. But our whole lives, every aspect of them, including our love life. It doesn't have to be conformed to the bipolar highs and lows of what we considered dating today. Our love lives do not have to be conformed to the onset mild disappointment sustained for years before relational implosion. It doesn't have to be conformed to the low-grade contentment almost each and every couple in America is settling for in this existence. There has to be something more than the levels of anxiety cohabitation instills. There has to something more.

This section is for all of you overthinkers; the obsessive-compulsive, always in-your-head people. For all of us who flat out have no idea what the Bible says about dating. And for everyone who doesn't know there is a God-sustained way to date compared to a *do-it-in-your-own-strength way*. To the people like me who had no idea that God has a will and a purpose not just for your life, but your love life as well. That he can use it, no matter how awful it's been, or how great it was, he can cause it to work together for good. For all of the Christians out there sick of the low-grade contentment and mid-level disappointment conforming to this world's way of dating has brought you. There is something more. Jesus didn't just promise life eternal, he also promised life abundant. And there is a way to transform your disappointment and low-grade contentment into something renewing. There is a possibility to actually discern and know what God is leading you to and from. And it all starts by seeking the Father's approval. I'll show you what I mean.

Chapter 1

The Gift of Singleness... Yeah Right!

[32] I want you to be free from the concerns of this life. An unmarried man can spend his time doing the Lord's work and thinking how to please him. [33] But a married man has to think about his earthly responsibilities and how to please his wife. [34] His interests are divided. In the same way, a woman who is no longer married or has never been married can be devoted to the Lord and holy in body and in spirit. But a married woman has to think about her earthly responsibilities and how to please her husband. [35] I am saying this for your benefit, not to place restrictions on you. I want you to do whatever will help you serve the Lord best, with as few distractions as possible. - 1 Corinthians 7:32-35

On our way to Bible study, one of my friends had an unusual pep in his step. His posture, that of a heroic protagonist. His resolve, chin up and hopeful. He wasn't the slumped down, *woe is me* figure any more. He found the answer to his problems... A girlfriend.

Even though his demeanor is a perfect example of what escaping singleness and getting in a relationship can do to a person. Don't we all as humans feel the same way when we find a potential significant other, a boyfriend, a girlfriend, or when we have a spectacular first date? Doesn't something click in us? We're more hopeful, more inspired, more eager to be optimistic about the future, more kind and loving to strangers, and more forgiving to a family member. In my friend's case, and in my experiences previous, this click or change, this spark of romance and shot of love kind of resembles an encounter with Jesus, or coming back to Jesus once again. It's energizing, it's inspiring. There's more love, more joy, more peace, more patience, more kindness, more goodness, more... Well, you get the point.

Why is it my friend had more fruit of the spirit from a new relationship than he did in his continuous relationship with Christ? Why is it that an unpredictable nineteen-year-old sophomore at junior college trumped the steadfast promises of Christ when it came to his outward character displayed by an inward resolve?

Don't be appalled. I'm sure deep down inside Christ is every Christian's hope and hope alone. But why is it that new relationships transform our inward resolve much more than our relationship with Jesus? Just like my friend.

For him, his deep seeded insecurities planted bitter roots needing acceptance from others. These bitter roots bore bitter fruit; fruit that dictated almost all of his actions. In the orchard of his walk with Christ, he's surrendered all of the tress of his life to Jesus, except this one. And that one facet of his life is a stronghold for the enemy. That facet is his dating life.

But let's get off our pedestals and examine the mire and muck of our lives underneath the artificial turf we claim is our glamorous lives on Instagram. In the wounds of my life, insecurities grew unchecked, hidden from the light of Christ. And the particular fruit it bore was the incapability of being alone with myself. Something I find in common with almost all individuals not yet healthy enough to endure a life-long relationship. I needed to be in a relationship. To have someone to focus all of my attention on, to fill my mind with, to give and receive all the love and affection I would ever need. In a sense, to be my Jesus.

Sure enough, when the reality set in for my friend's girlfriend; the reality that her deep seeded insecurities not yet given to Jesus wouldn't be fixed by a boyfriend. When she discovered her insecurities we're just powder-coated over with superficial feelings for someone else. When the reality set in that her insecurities are still consuming her alive under the surface, she opted out of that relationship. And my friend's joy, and hope and peace went with her.

This takes us back to 1 Corinthians 7, out of all the relational advice that's been misconstrued over the centuries these verses take the cake. Christ followers were, and were even more so about to start being tortured, killed, and boiled alive in the thousands at the colosseum. Of course getting married as a Christ follower might not have been the best idea to rush into back then. But I do believe these verses paint a vivid picture every unmarried believer should reflect on.

Being married now for almost a year, even in this brief time, I can tell you is a night and day difference from the single-mindedness towards Christ the apostle Paul is describing. Before I ever bumped into my future wife, I spent two years without a girlfriend. The first year I didn't even think about dating or feel like had had God's approval to do so. I, as Paul said, started to spend my time thinking about how to please the Lord. Something I never thought of once before in the twenty-two years I lived. I thought about how to serve God, a lot. I mean, what else is there to do when you're committed to *not* finding the one, not playing video games, and not looking at porn?

I thought about Christ. I thought about me. I thought about what Christ was to me, and what I was to him. Who I was meant to be, and what he had meant for me. You know, those deep seeded questions about life. Questions like why am I here, and what is my purpose? Like verse thirty-two mentions, I was finally free from the main concerns my brokenness had instilled, not being alone. And I had the chance to jump into the fast lane of soul searching and had the single focus to do so.

I focused on Christ; I surrendered all of my life to him, no bitter roots lefts un-inspected. And by searching the face of the Father, I found myself. Who I was as his child, a child of God adopted by the blood of Jesus spilled on that cross for you and me. To sacrifice himself as he saved us from the car wreck of this existence.

When I discovered who I am, I was ready to look for who I wanted to be with. Once I discovered who I was in Christ and detoxed from everything this world instilled in me, I finally felt like our Father gave me the approval to start dating again.

Individual Devotional (15 Minutes)

1) When it comes to what the apostle Paul had mentioned as a divided interest, have you ever given serious thought or attention to pleasing God? What are the specific ways you have done or not done this before?

2) How can you begin to meditate and reflect on *doing the Lord's work*? What would that commitment look like daily, weekly and monthly?

3) In verse 35, Paul explains he's not saying all this to be legalistic and place restrictions on anyone, but to do whatever will help us serve the Lord best with as few distractions as possible; have you ever dated to distract your mind from the sting of loneliness?

   a) How might this have hindered your relationship with God?

Couples Devotional (15 Minutes)

1) Have you surrendered your dating life to Christ?

   a) How can you tell? Did that look like a prayer, a self-commitment, a conversation?

2) Do you know any couples that try to fill the deep voids of their lives and emptiness with each other, instead of Christ?

   a) How has that been working out for them?

3) What are some issues in your life that this relationship isn't fixing like you thought it might?

   a) How can you start to find true healing?

4) How often is your focus more about pleasing each other relationally, than pleasing Christ?

5) What bitter roots and insecurities might be affecting you today from the past? What would you close friends identify them as? In other words, what hurts from the past still sting today and possibly hinder your life in some way?

Application
Make some time these next few mornings, reflect on how you can start *pleasing the lord* in your life. Figure out what that looks like daily, weekly, and monthly, and write it down on a monthly planner or a monthly calendar.

Chapter 2

Signs Are For The Wicked...

[29] As the crowd pressed in on Jesus, he said, "This evil generation keeps asking me to show them a miraculous sign. But the only sign I will give them is the sign of Jonah. [30] What happened to him was a sign to the people of Nineveh that God had sent him. What happens to the Son of Man will be a sign to these people that he was sent by God."
- Luke 4:29-30

Coming to Christ was definitely a sobering experience for me. I let go of drinking every day, I let go of porn, and I even let go of trying to find *the one*. After a year of not even considering dating or girlfriends or relationships, just focusing on God alone, I finally felt like I had the green light to start looking again. Not because I couldn't handle being alone anymore. Actually, once I had surrendered every part of my life and invited Christ to come in and renew my mind, I spent a ton of time by myself. But I actually never felt completely alone, or lonely like I did in previous seasons of singleness without Christ. And finally, after some tremendously deep healing that needed to take place in the furthest recesses of my heart, I believe God gave me the metaphorical thumbs up to *go get 'em slugger*!

Which lead me to the place every single person gets to when they're ready to find the one, *now what*!? I'm twenty-two, on fire for Christ and don't know any Christian girls I'd like to pursue. So I did what I think most single Christians do, pray, and pray, and pray again. But that didn't work. She didn't just fall from the sky on my lap in a wedding dress. So I did what other single Christians do, I went to a cool college ministry to find some single college girls. If you don't have an over the top awesome college ministry at your church don't worry, neither did I. Instead, I drove thirty plus minutes and two cities over to find a church that did. And if you still don't have a cool college ministry like that anywhere near you just join Christian Mingle; it's pretty much the same thing but online. I joke, of course.

Which takes me back to single, twenty-two year old me. The stars were aligning. Christ had healed my heart and renewed my mind. I was able to date from a place of being complete in God, not empty and searching for an earthly substitute. I submerged myself volunteering in a ministry where I was sure to find a hottie. I enrolled in twelve full units to increase my odds of having a few cuties in my classes. I played it off cool and *low-key* informed my friends I'm back on the market and ready to be set up with their gorgeous friends. Or I probably posted a desperate cry for attention on Facebook. You know, either or. And I got to the place you've gotten to time and time again, *now what God!?*

How many times have you gotten to that *now what* place with God like I did? I'm single and ready to Christian mingle, now what do I do God? I've declared my status as single on social media, I've enrolled and enlisted in everything possible to meet cute girls besides interpretive jazz dance class, and yet there is not an abundance of potential future-wifeys that I can choose from just lurking about! I was waiting on God, waiting for him to open a door. And when no door opened, I went from hopeful in Christ to infuriated with God in two-point-eight weeks flat.

Mrs. Right didn't sit right next to me in class. She didn't come up and introduce herself at Starbucks, where I chose to study six nights a week instead of my room because random cute girls don't just walk into my room like they do Starbucks. My friends you say? Not a single useful one seemed to know any *Mrs. Perfects* just lying around waiting to meet me, their future hubby. And most frustrating of all, God didn't slow motion any *perfect* moments to catch a glimpse of the right girl like he does in all of those romance movies.

I was looking, praying, asking, seeking and knocking, but she and God sure as heck didn't make it obvious. Why is it that when you're not looking, or you're not dating, it seems like there is a plethora of potential boyfriends or girlfriends just grazing about your pond. Yet when you are single and ready to mingle, they've all flown south for the winter?

I believe the ancient Jews in Jesus' day and age could probably relate to the way I was feeling when it came to finding the *promised one* of God. We were both under tyrannical occupation; Israel to the Romans, myself to the pent up hormonal necessities to mate, I mean find a mate. Their God wasn't doing miraculous things anymore and the so called *messiah* or *promised one* was nowhere to be found. Whereas my life was just as bland and void of potential. Sure, I make a ridiculous connection here, but still, you know what it's like looking for the *promised one* to deliver you from your hardships of singleness. It is agonizing.

However, I would say more difficult than having no potential match come around is actually bumping into one, or two or twenty. Can you relate? When you see him or her and your heart starts to flutter, what do you do? When your friend starts telling you about a potential match you *have* to meet, what then? When you strike up that conversation with a complete stranger (which is crucial because initiating conversation is half the battle), how do you go from there to sitting at a table for two? When you get together for that first initial cup of coffee, which is a necessity for dating because of its non-intimidating, informal, easy invitation, how will you know? Are there any overthinkers out there like me? *Now what God!?*

Well, believe it or not, the ancient Jews of Jesus' day and age had a ton of potential *Mr. Rights* lurking about as their future messiah. One after another as a matter of fact. Is he the right one? Or is it this guy? He could be the right one, but have you seen his teeth? By the time Jesus got on scene the religious rulers had given up on the next miracle maker being the real *Mr. right messiah*. Finally, they did what most of us believers do when we're burnt out on finding the right one; they demand a sign from God.

"Give me a sign God" is what I'd cry out to him after every single coffee date. "I don't like this about her or that, but God if this is your will and doing give me a sign, I don't know what you want." And I never understood why Jesus told the Jews only a wicked generation requires a sign. It seems like a pretty practical way to eliminate the search and figure out what God wants. Until the day I actually got a sign.

I had met a girl, a cute Christian girl, and coffee went good, real good. So I started praying for a sign like I did with the dozen or so other girls I went to Starbucks with. "She has to be the one! Right God?" I'd think to myself. And hour after hour once we departed from that coffee date I was racking my brain, "Is she the right one? Give me a sign!" Until finally, a few days later, after my morning workout, I became totally defeated because God hadn't given me a sign to continue to pursue her or not, and I got pissed off. "I dedicated my life to you God and this is all you got for me? Silence? If you really loved us, your children, like you say you do, you would give me a sign whether or not she is the right one for me and if I should ask her out to dinner." And at 6:02am as I am turning on the hot water in the shower, sitting on the edge of the tub, complaining/praying for God to give me a sign in tears of frustration, at 6:03am my entire house began to shake and tremble...

Well, every house did in my neighborhood. It was an earthquake, most of So-Cal felt it. But could it be? No way! Was this a sign? Could this have been the sign I was praying for!? I honestly don't know and chances are *probably not*! But I can tell you this, at 6:02 I prayed for God to give me a sign if she is the right one or not. At 6:03 So-Cal had a minor earthquake. And by 6:04 I realized only a wicked generation would ask for a sign, because signs are empty.

Signs deplete the life of faith with empty substitutes of favor. You don't have to continue to search and seek God's heart and will if you can look at any old coincidence and call it a sign of favor. It's empty, because signs are what you make them out to be. And after the earthquake, I was more confused than ever! I didn't know what to make of it. I was dumbstruck, babbling my prayers out. "...Father, thank you for the sign... or maybe that wasn't a sign... but either way that was pretty cool... but was that a sign of *yes* I will move mountains for your love? Or was that a sign of no, doom and destruction will befall your way if you continue to pursue her?" And on that day I realized, I don't need a sign. I need faith. Faith that Jesus would organically led me where I needed to go with who I needed to be with. I needed faith in him, not in empty signs I could misconstrue the way I want. Maybe that's why Jesus said only a wicked generation would ask for a sign. Because it's an empty substitute for having faith in our Father, constantly searching his heart and seeking his approval and will.

Life in this kind of faith is not easy though. Relying on Jesus to lead you from one step to the next, throughout each and every day of your life by his spirit's nudging can be pretty hard. I guess signs would seem to make things easier on paper. And Jesus in his kindness did promise that wicked generation a sign. He promised them the sign of Jonah. And sure enough, he descended into the depths below, and just like Jonah, rose again three days later. But as I discovered, and as the ancient Israelites proved, signs are empty. I was no better off for it, and neither were they. I ended up even more confused, and they still refused to follow and pursue their *promised one* even when God did hand-deliver him with a sign. Trust me; you don't need a sign, just keep your faith in Jesus. Follow the spirit's prompting in your life. Flee from temptation, and God will get you where you need to go. Even if you are being swallowed by a few whales of dating-hardship, we have a good, good Father and he will lead you to his will. You'll know if you have his approval, the veil has been torn, and you can come boldly to his throne to find mercy and grace. Try to enjoy the mysteries of today, because he has been in your tomorrow, and will safely get you where you need to be.

Individual Devotional (15 Minutes)

1) How much time in your daily routine currently goes to spending time with God and focusing on him alone?

2) Can you honestly say you are dating from a place of being *whole* in Christ, or are there some specific areas he needs to bring healing to?

3) How many times have you gotten to that *now what* place with God?

4) What are/were some of the hardest parts of being single to you?

5) Is there a marker, a resolution you can look back on and say yes, I have given my dating and relationship life to Christ?

   a) How could *not* surrendering that aspect of your life in faith be affecting the other areas of your faith?

Couples Devotional (15 Minutes)

1) What were some of the signs you might have been looking for from God to get together with each other?

   a) Do you feel like God provided what you hoped to see, or did it feel more like a step of faith asking out and dating one another?

2) How are you as a couple pursuing our Father's approval together?

3) What areas of your current relationship reflect doing it God's way?

   a) What areas don't?

4) How can dating with the Father's approval in mind change your

   relationship or improve it?

Application

Write down the major and minor aspects of your life, from school to work, from social life to dating. Write down the different areas of your life. After reviewing these, are any areas of your life not surrendered to Christ? Meaning you do it your way and keep God out of it. Take this next week and pray and surrender them to Him. Wrestle with why you haven't already, and entrust every area of your life to your Heavenly Father.

Chapter 3

The Dating X-Factor

[28] And we know that God causes everything to work together for the good of those who love God and are called according to his purpose for them. - Romans 8:28

Before I started to value my relationship with Jesus I would always pray something like this, "God, this is what I want. I really want it, so please bless me with it and please bless my decisions..." But something happened when I started to trust him and have faith in his love for me. And from that time on my prayers sounded more like, "Father what do you want for me, please let your will and plans be done." And when it comes to dating, I bet some of us have overthought this idea of what God wants and who he wants us to be with and if he approves of the one we're currently with. Society calls them the one that *fate* or the *universe* has in store, but we know God is greater than the universe, he made it. So does he approve, are they the right one? Or are some of us blocking this thought from our head all together because we know the answer already... He's been in jail five times and is going on six; maybe he ain't the one honey.

But what about those on the flip side of this spectrum and don't really know? Does God really care about the incessant details of our love lives? Doesn't he know the plans he has for us, and is working things out according to his will? So why do anything? Won't fate just take care of it? Do I really need to pray if this is a good idea to stay with him, or pursue her, or break it off with them? Does God really care? How do we know, what's the x-factor?

Well, I believe God cares about every detail of our lives, including dating and two stories might paint this picture better for us. The first is mine, and the second is my friend Chris'. But let's start with mine. After twenty plus coffee dates and more nightmare stories than the *Tales from the Crypt*, I was going into spring semester pretty defeated. As I walked to and fro all of my new spring classes, the good looking girls on campus just didn't appeal like they used too. Because, after twenty plus coffee dates I realized, they might be very attractive, but that doesn't mean they're very faith-filled. Not exactly the *go get 'em slugger* attitude I started with. But then I sat next to *her* in my English class.

She was cute, but not really my type. So several weeks went by and we'd small talk, nothing big. And then one day on the way to the library before class, there she was, just chilling right outside on a bench. And I threw up a little one of those half prayers, you know like "Should I talk to her or do homework? Father, what do you want?" Of course homework lost that battle. And after forty-five minutes of talking we had to walk from the library to our class before it started. As we sat there in English I saw her in a whole new light. Of course I did, we just talked for forty-five minutes! We talked about school and class and sports and music and faith, and it turns out she was a Christ follower too. This definitely sparked a fire of interest that shed new light on her possibility of being *the one*.

With twenty plus failed coffee dates propelling the anticipation that she might finally be *the one* God was leading me too, I put my game face on. I sprang into action after class got out, and sprung up behind her with serial killer-like surprise, startling her with an awkward "Hey!" And after taking time to un-startle her, I asked like a normal human being if she would like to go get coffee with me before or after class some time. She said yes.

The next story, Chris' story, involves two people, Chris and Alice. Chris and Alice were two typical twenty-somethings. They went to church, went to school, went to work, lived and had fun. They worked in the same office building and they'd often float over to each other's department for small talk and flirting. Well, it's a small world after all and the friendships formed with others at work eventually lead them to the same parties together. Side note, if you're looking for *the one* as a Christian, she probably isn't the one getting hammered at the party. And for months they would harmlessly flirt. Which lead to harmless late night texting. Which lead to harmless parties with each other. Which after months, harmfully lead to this night. They had beer, alone time and un-sedated hormones. They left the party together and went someplace a little more, quiet...

There is no official word on what happened that night. But Chris let the situation get too far with a girl he wasn't too crazy for. He let her desires control the night. And in his attempts to fix the mess he made, he stopped talking to her, stopped seeing her at work and stopped hanging out with her all together. What Chris didn't know was that Alice was quite the head-case. Immensely deep daddy-issues, deep rooted insecurities and intense narcissism had all been bottled up in a vacuum of self-defeat for four years and counting. But he didn't know that. All he knew was how far they went romantically wasn't where he wanted to be with her. And thinking he was doing the right thing by completely pulling away; felt more like pulling the rug right out from under her. Maybe he thought he can avoid reaping what he sowed, all I know is that he scorned her. And you know what they say about hell and women scorn...

With raising hell in mind, she began to twist and retell the story of that night to her friends. Well, first to her friends, and then to their coworkers and then to anyone who would see her Facebook posts. Yet the story she told wasn't the one Chris explained happened. The story she told claimed Chris had sexually assaulted her that night. And all hell did break loose. That night she bragged about at first with her friends; she now flipped when Chris pulled back, sparking her insecurity fire into a lunatic inferno. And looking back now, I wonder if where Chris ended up that night was where his Heavenly Father wanted him to be? I wonder if his Heavenly Father approved?

The difference between those two stories in my mind is the smallest prayer you might have ever heard, "Father what do you want?" I asked that question before I talked to *her*. I asked that question before I asked her to coffee; I asked for his approval before our first, second, third and fourth date. <u>Giving him the option of closing the door not only gave me God's approval in my mind since he didn't, but encouraged me to keep moving forward</u>. Giving him control over our dating, to shut the door if she wasn't the one, freed me up to pursue her without the overthinking. Giving God control and seeking his approval to keep moving forward is the Dating X-Factor.

I wonder if Chris would have kept moving forward with Alice if he would have stopped and thought, "Father, what do you want?" Would the story of his life have gone to that dark chapter and its repercussions thereof? If Chris would have asked God before they flirted at work day after day for months, "Is this right?" If Chris would have prayed before they started to hang out every weekend and party, "Father is this what you want?" If Chris would have straight up stopped what he was doing, put down the drink and asked God, "Father do you approve?" Before he drove off to be alone with her, would the Holy Spirit have screamed out at him "STOP! What are you doing!? STOP!" Those moments may have felt good, but his life is still recovering.

Something good always happens when you love God and live your life in his will, constantly searching for the purpose we're called to. As Romans 8:28 says, he works all things together for good. I can't say the same for those living outside the framework of scripture, yes, even for those who call themselves Christians but don't live like it as Chris and Alice reassuringly don't. But God does work all things for good according to those who love him and live their lives with his calling and purpose. Including the heart-wrenching disappointment of *her* not actually being *the one*.

The Father's approval, or at least giving it up to him, makes all the difference. It's the safety net, the guiding compass, the X-Factor of dating. Here's a little glimpse of why I know this to be true. Why I believe dating in a Christ-honoring way can change your life.

Now like Chris' story, my story also ends in disappointment. I never even speak to *her* again. But we had a great coffee date. A great first date. A great second, third and fourth date. It was the best April in a while. A bright month in two years. Yet, I'll never forget coming home from leading a middle school retreat the last weekend in April. She didn't talk to me that whole weekend. As a matter of fact she didn't talk to me all of Spring Break that week. Not responding to any communication from me at all. Which lead to a very awkward first day back in class.

The instructor dismissed us, class had ended, and she sprinted out of those doors. She sprinted as if I was in fact a serial killer out to get her, but like all horror movies, I caught up. I caught up and asked if she was ok... After a long moment she broke down crying in the middle of the parking lot. Sobbing, all she could say was "I'm sorry." She explained to me that her childhood friend, her best friend and high school sweetheart lost his battle with drugs and killed himself. The kid she tried to get plugged into church and encounter Christ, just died. And she was too emotionally wrecked to be in a relationship with me. It felt like a train hit me as her words sped forth from her mouth.

Yet the weirdest thing happened. Every single anxiety, fear and hurt I gained from our lack of communication the week prior just seemed to melt away. Every single disappointed feeling in me knowing this was it seemed to vanish. Instead, I looked at her intently, smiled and said "Everything will be ok." Her tears were interrupted by surprise at my demeanor. "You mean you're not upset?" she asked. I asked her what kind of Christ follower would I be if I only cared about her as a potential wife, and didn't continue to care about what's best for her, even if that's not with me? Even if that meant the end of us, and another failed opportunity of finding the one. For the record I had no idea what was coming out of my mouth, things that deep never surfaced in *old Tyler's* life. But she was comforted, and extremely relieved she could morn in this time of loss without any added guilt or grief by me.

I never saw her again. But all that weakness and insecurity I felt after camp never came back. God gave me his strength. And a few days later after that parking lot closure, she sent me two texts. The first was a frantic text. The family of the departed needed a verse for the memorial and asked her to supply one since she was the closest Christian the family knew. And after fifty verses later, and an hour of my work day, elation! She found the perfect verse that touched her heart and went on to comfort and minister to the family. After that set of texts arrived a final text, it went something like this.

> I never told you this, but one year after breaking up with my high school sweetheart I finally prayed. And that day before class, I walked out of my car and over to the library. And on that particular day I prayed as I walked up to the building and I asked God to bring me a nice Christian man. And right after I sat down in front of the library, here you came out of nowhere. Thank you...

Through dating I got a chance to inspire someone closer to Jesus. I was given the chance to reaffirm that our Father was a good, good Father who hears his children. Even the furthest ones from him. And yes, even through a failed relationship God can work all things together for good. He can work pain and hurt and disappointment out to inspire a struggling girl, strengthen a young man's resolve, and minister to a family in mourning by Jesus' words, "Come to me all you tired and heavy burdened and will give you rest." That's the verse she chose. And a few months later, after patient endurance had its way, when I wasn't even looking, I would find *the one*.

Individual Devotional (15 Minutes)

1) Does the majority of your prayer life sound like "God this is what I want" or "God help me know what you want for me?" Take some time and reflect on what it consists of.

2) Do you think God almighty actually cares about who we end up with? Why or why not?

   a) Could God actually care more about our dating lives than we do?

3) How often have you left God out of the decision and just did what you thought was best?

   a) Is this an ongoing pattern? Think about the last few months and reflect.

4) How has dating and *doing it your way* in your past relationships turned out?

   a) Do you think by following God he can lead you to something better?

Couples Devotional (15 Minutes)

1) From the way we're carrying out our relationship, do you think God approves of the way we're doing things?

   a) Why or why not?

2) Have we both come together and just taken a moment in prayer or in conversation and surrendered control of our relationship to Jesus?

   a) What's stopping you from this dating *X-Factor*?

3) How is our relationship lined up with the confines of scripture? How is it not?

   a) How can you we seek counsel on this if needed?

4) When it comes to God working all things out together for good, how can the failures of our past influence us to do things his way this time around?

Application

Together, find a Christ following couple you know who is married and ask them if you can get lunch soon, ask them for some guidance in the areas you might be struggling with or have questions about.

Chapter 4

A Match Made In Heaven

[10] This is what the LORD says: "You will be in Babylon for seventy years. But then I will come and do for you all the good things I have promised, and I will bring you home again. [11] For I know the plans I have for you," says the LORD. "They are plans for good and not for disaster, to give you a future and a hope. [12] In those days when you pray, I will listen. [13] If you look for me wholeheartedly, you will find me. [14] I will be found by you," says the LORD... - Jeremiah 29:10-14
Also read Ezekiel 20:4-8

After twenty plus coffee dates and now a failed potential relationship, I stopped worrying about finding the one in my own effort. Sure, that looked like sitting in my room every night binging on Netflix. But after seeing how God came through in that last situation truly reassured me. I guess I just knew God would continue to work things out like he always does.

But some questions did come to my mind as a habitual overthinker. What if she was the one? What if she was the one I was made for? What if she was my only true shot at happiness in this existence? What if she was my soul mate but Satan used a tragedy to ensure we'd break up and now my life is ruined forever and ever? I mean if that was my soul mate and one true chance at a real gratifying love, I'm screwed.

What about you? Have you ever thought you found the one? You know the one you're going to marry and fly off into the sunset with, yet that plane would later come down crashing and burning. Have you ever told someone you know they're the one you're going to marry? What about stories like my friend's old youth pastor who discovered his wife cheating on him? Was she ever his soul mate, or was it just a lie to begin with?

Well I encourage you to find the verse or two where the term soulmate is presented and identified and clearly explained. But here's a time saver, there isn't one. Now before the unhinged romantic in you throws this book or tablet into a fire let me reassure you. There is no scripture indicating you have a single once in a lifetime partner that is your only chance for deep connection and love at an ecstasy-level that you can experience with only them and never come down from. I mean what if they got hit by a bus before you ever met, or moved to Antarctica? You're doomed for life if your soul mate was your only shot. Does that sound like an all sovereign, grace filled, second chance giving God?

But in God's grace, the ancient Jews in accordance to scripture's consistency did believe in matches made in Heaven. And this should free some of you like it did me. It's a testament to Jesus' grace. No matter how screwed up you were or your old life was, with Jesus the best is yet to come. And God has a person in mind for you. Someone that he doesn't just approve of, but will move mountains for you two. A match made in heaven.

It doesn't matter who you are or what you've done, God's got a plan for you. Even if your sin has lead you to a life collapsing in around you, like the ancient city of Jerusalem crumbling down to the ground because of sin's toll. God's message to his children then, applies to us today. He knows the plans he has for you. And although a previous thing may have crumbled, his plans are for good and not for evil. Even as your life drags forward from the ashes and ruins of relational devastation. God can work all things together for good! And as romanticized and great-in-theory a soulmate may be; when it comes to that last fling, that three year relationship, a failed engagement, ten years of cohabitation, you name it, it's time as the apostle Paul said to "Focus on this one thing: Forgetting the past and looking forward to what lies ahead."

These verses in Jeremiah twenty-nine are pretty incredible verses. They are some of the most popular in Christendom, yet immensely short-changed. The prophet Jeremiah probably had one of the hardest gigs in the bible. He was constantly telling the Israelites in Jerusalem to repent of their sins, turn to God, and obey his commandments, or else God would deliver the city to a foreign nation that would destroy it brick by brick. Yet sure enough the people listened to the more popular prophets who said it's all good, just do you, go after what you want, truth is what you make it. A message still pretty popular today. And Jeremiah was there when the people, time after time, repeated the same mistakes, the same sin as before, saying they believe in God but lived a different lifestyle.

Sure enough, as Jeremiah testified to, we reap what we sow. And so did Jerusalem. The enemy army surrounded their city. They starved them out. People turned to cannibalism, parents eating children, people eating people. And finally when the people were begging, pleading for death, their wishes were granted. And the Babylonians conquered the city, raped the women, killed the men, enslaved the children, burned the city to ground and took who was ever left into captivity and slavery. And it's after these events that Jeremiah utters these words from God, "I know the plans I have for you (talking about the Israelite people), they're plans for good and not for evil, plans to prosper you and not to harm you." Other translations say to give you a hope and a future. Popular verses indeed, but profoundly unfathomed compared to what Jeremiah saw and lived. This specific promise may have been just for them, but let's note the patterns of their journey, take to heart God's similar promises to us, and avoid the mistakes they made in their faith journey.

The Israelite journey has been the same since leaving Egypt. Let me sum it up. God saves them, they worship God, time would pass, they begin to worship other priorities over God, they abandon God, they experience the hardships of life without God, and they turn back to God. God saves them, they worship God, time would pass, they begin to worship other priorities over God, and they abandon God... and round and round again for millennia. This is the sin-cycle. And it's prevalent from the moments after Moses takes them through the Red Sea. It's rehearsed time and time again after Joshua departs and the judges come and go. It's alive and unfortunately well from when King David leaves Solomon in charge, and all throughout the future divided kingdom of Israel. First, the Northern Kingdom continues their sins from the past, as God mentions, "They rebelled against me and would not listen. They did not get rid of the vile images they were obsessed with, or forsake the idols of Egypt" (Ezekiel 20:8). And the northern tribes are wiped off the face of the map. Then finally, as all tail spins comes to a crash and burn moment; Judah, the Southern Kingdom, continued their sins from the past, and God let their entire existence obliterate under the fists of a foreign nation. Removing everything they once were.

What about our lives today? Is God delivering us from our singleness, only for us to fall back into the sin-cycle? How many times will we as God's people build the city of our lives on Christ, yet let sexual immorality and other idols destroy the things we've built. Will this next relationship burn down to the ground like the last one did? Sure the circumstances are different, but the lesson is the same. Jesus has that match for you. The person he wants you to spend the rest of your life with, the person that was seemingly made just for you and you for them. But His grace and deliverance comes with a choice. Will you obey this time? Will you follow Christ? You know, intentionally building on the solid foundation of Jesus first in your lives. Foreign concept in today's world I know. But when you trust in what God says, and build your life on the foundation he's laid out, your relationship can hold against any battle or oppression.

Or will you repeat the sin-cycle one more time around and fall prey to our sinful desires, then fall captive to reaping what you sowed. Continuously wasting year after year, relationship after relationship, opportunity after opportunity. Emotionally, mentally and spiritually draining all that you are. It's our choice. And no matter what the rubble of your life looks like; relationally desolate in hindsight or blissfully ignorant to the sin-cycle now, Jesus can break the chains that bind and take you off of the road of relational destruction.

You have grace in Christ. You have God's unmerited favor! Your next first kiss can be your last first kiss. Your next first date can be your last first date. And you can continuously move onto better places in life with them. We don't have to live in the past or live with regret. He knows the plans he has for us. He does have a seemingly perfect match that you've inadvertently been moving toward your whole life. But grace is a gift, we have to choose it. If you're single, your Father isn't holding your match made in heaven back from you because he doesn't approve of your past, he's bringing them closer to him so you can find them there when you find his embrace. The Father has an approved time for you and your special someone, don't go the long way around in the desert of hard lessons, flee from temptation and run to faith in him.

Individual Devotional (15 Minutes)

1) Did you ever think in a past relationship that you had found the one?

   a) How'd it end? Can any part of the sin-cycle be represented in what happened?

2) Where did you first hear of this idea of a soulmate in your life? How does this free you knowing it's more like a match made in heaven, instead of a one time all or nothing?

3) Reflect honestly, is there a pattern of sin in your relationships or life that keeps bringing destruction? Destruction to your finances, relationships, aspirations, etc.?

4) Looking back, how many opportunities have you let crumble because you did it *your way*? What are you going to different in the future? When can you start?

Couples Devotional (15 Minutes)

1) How has your idea of a soul mate shifted?

   a) How might it have affected your dating life before?

2) What are somethings or some people (old friends, ex's, etc.) you need to leave in the past and move forward like the apostle Paul said?

   a) Why might this be hard for you to let go of?

3) What are some of the ways you are building your relationship on Christ's foundation?

4) Do you have any couple-friends in your life that built their relationship on Christ?

   a) What's stopping you from asking them to pour into your life today and help you along this dating journey?

Application

When it comes to sinful patterns in our lives, look at how you spend your money, your free time, and past relationships. Is how you've dated, spent your money and free time aligned with scripture? What are the things we need to start doing to align our lives with his word?

Chapter 5

"Missionary Dating"

[14] Don't team up with those who are unbelievers. How can righteousness
be a partner with wickedness? How can light live with darkness?
- 2 Corinthians 6:14
Also read 1 Corinthians 6:12-20 / 1 Corinthians 7:36 /
1 Corinthians 7:12-16

There are numerous amounts of blogs on the internet, sermons preached on podcast and just all around chatter on the topic of missionary or missional dating. For the prodigals like me who have no idea what missionary dating was or is; in a sense, missionary or missional dating is the intentional pursuit by a Christ follower after an individual who does not believe in God, or is far from God—in order to both date them and convert them—or simply lead them closer to Christ. Sounds perfectly harmless and like good intentions, right? But above are some scriptures that argue against missionary dating.

Scripture clearly indicates to not intentionally date unbelievers. Making it clear, our Father does not approve of the idea. However, God being a good Father, also lays some foundation for those who are currently in a relationship with unbelievers and or are married to them. Or given today's context, the relationships in which we have been living together for years and now have children which can pretty much be in a category next marriage without the title (so put a ring on it if that's you). There is a multitude of personal discernment that every person needs to meditate on individually, and let the Holy Spirit speak to you about.

Either way, there is a ton of black, a ton of white, or even more grey. I don't want to be another voice amongst the chatter. I don't want to strike strong and hard with my opinion and entrench you deeper in yours. So here are two stories that hit close to my heart.

The first is with my friend Alex and Christy. Alex was a pastor's kid who considered himself a Christian, yet found himself in the same deep ruts unbelievers find themselves in. He was working at a local restaurant when Christy walked in for the first time. Alex was pretty strong in faith, even though he hadn't surrendered every part of his life to Jesus.

Nonetheless, he was still bold in the faith he did have and liked talk to people about Jesus. Christy was the opposite. Christy hated *religion* and religious people. Not because she was a bad person, but because religious people have treated her awfully for the life decisions she's made. On paper, they were a match made in hell. And as a matter of fact, the first time Christy saw Alex, she had one thing in mind... My first and only advice to Alex would have been to run away from this girl and never look back.

The next story still rips me up on the inside. A dear friend, Ashley, hit yet another low point in her life. Someone I have known since high school hit bottom in her faith and has stayed there. She's a beautiful, bright, spirit-lead girl who's loved Jesus since the time she was little. But just like the Old Testament illustrations for the New Testament sin-cycle/struggle. She faced her share of struggles being a beautiful girl with faith. She had a heart for Christ, but a passion for the party. She did both in high school. Some months she'd be whole and strong in Jesus, other months she'd be in another boy's bed. It was a constant battle. But after high school she got off the sidelines of faith and into the game serving in student ministry. And there, serving in student ministry, she met her *match made in heaven*. The things God was working together for them were incredible to see, almost fairy tale like.

But they didn't live happily ever after. As a matter of fact, they didn't even have a single date. Yet again, weak, passive Christian men failed another girl. He didn't have the stones to ask her out, only enough to flirt for months. Instead, he let an over-aggressive sophomore in Bible College on the fringe of lunacy in light of not receiving a ring last spring semester ask him out and ask him to be her boyfriend. After their months of flirting and hints Ashley kept dropping, she felt immensely rejected and out-casted by this recent turn of events. And it didn't help the situation that this girl hated Ashley for her new boyfriend's previous interest in her. She was the odd girl out amongst the volunteers. And her circumstances in the church soon followed. A few weeks later she met a guy at her junior college. And he wasn't passive about his desires or the sex appeal he saw. Once again she left the church for the party and another boy.

Back to the first couple, as unabashedly as Christy's desires were for Alex, she didn't expect what Alex's counter-offer was. Instead of going to a bar sometime, he suggested a Bible study over coffee. She wanted lust, but he gave her coffee and scripture. He ditched the scriptural mandates and went in holy guns blazing.

I knew this thing would fall part, crash, and burn in disaster for the both of them. I knew as a matter of fact that she'd never believe but simply try on faith as she tried to be with him, abandoning both when things got bad. But something happened that I did not expect. I was wrong. And even though they aren't together anymore, months later she's still learning about this whole faith thing.

Unfortunately, what's worse than being wrong; is being right when you don't want to be. Ashley chased the boy who intentionally pursued her (go figure guys); she chased him all the way to his one bedroom apartment. She used to post how incredible winter retreat was, but now she posts how great Cabo was over spring break. I know she loves the Lord still, it just hurts to think things could've ended up differently if we as Christ followers knew what God actually has to say about chasing unbelievers. Doesn't scripture rhetorically ask "How can righteousness be a partner with wickedness? How can light live with darkness?" Or in today's context, how can a Christ follower sign a rental lease with someone who blatantly denies their Lord is real?

When it comes to missional dating I don't know what to tell you in your current relationship specifically. I know God is God and I am not. And when our opinions differ from his, I trust that he is right and I am wrong. So I don't believe there is a one size fit all answer when it comes to your current circumstances. This is probably why the apostle Paul goes into immense detail about all the variances. But I can tell you this, if your future possible relationship is going to tear you away from Christ, you probably won't have your Father's approval. Why would he be excited for something that will tear you away and keep you from him? As a child of God, isn't that what our lives are all about? Being one with the father as Christ is?

What if this concept were to be applied to your earthly father if you had or have one that's always treated you right? What if you were to intentionally invest your whole heart, and time and finances into an individual who despises your earthly father? Someone who hates the fact you talk to him. Who would give anything for you to never speak his name again. Would you really invest everything you are into a person like that? Than why would we put a title on that type of relationship and intentionally go after them if you're single and excuse why it's ok?

I don't think your earthly father would approve of that person if they caught wind of this scheme. And maybe that's why our Heavenly Father who knows all things, and knows all hearts speaks through the apostle Paul and says, "A woman is bound to her husband as long as he lives. But if her husband dies, she is free to marry anyone she wishes, but he must belong to the Lord." And the same applies to men. If you're single and ready to mingle, you're risking so much if they're not a Christ follower by more than words. I don't believe God's trying to ruin your odds at love; I simply believe he is good enough and all-powerful enough to bring you a Christ follower you're immensely attracted to. I believe he is great enough to work through your current love, and bring your current boyfriend or girlfriend to him. But don't make the mistake; no one makes a fool of God who knows the intentions of your heart. Don't chase people with sinking ships of faith, they'll plunge you down with them.

Looking back I'm glad I didn't take up the added burden of missionary dating. I had just experienced my first failed dating relationship and was approximately six months away from meeting my match made in heaven, my future wife. And it seemed like Satan knew this too. What was once a dry well of interest in me seemed to overflow overnight! And all the wrong girls from the past and the obviously wrong girls from the now started to come out of the woodwork! I definitely think this was supernatural opposition, since I had a beard down to my chest at this time to scare away all the hood rats. Yet they still came. And I could have taken the missional dating approach. I could have spent the rest of my life burdened with two impossible situations; spending all my hours on the battlefields of faith pointing people to Jesus out in the world, only to come home to a bloodier war of trying to lead my spouse and kids to Jesus too in my house. War on both fronts kills even the greatest of armies. Just ask every toppled army who ever had to fight one. I could have spent my life teaching others about faith and Jesus outside of the house, and constantly try to preach about faith and Jesus inside my house too. But as Jesus said, "A kingdom divided will fall," and a divided focus primarily results in two incomplete foundations, both unable to endure the test of time. Is that pursuit something worth risking the sanctity of your soul over and the eternity of your future children?

I don't know what to tell you. Unfortunately I do see so many Christ followers reciprocating these pursuits for all the wrong reasons;

loneliness, insecurities, fear and a general lack of trust that he's a good Father. And it's so worth the wait. Stay lonely, live in your room off of Top Romen and Netflix at night. Fight the good fight. <u>Have faith that the person God has for you is great looking and loves Christ like you do</u>. Don't settle, they're worth the wait! Maybe God is stretching or pressing you now so you can surrender these last few parts of your life to him and be ready for *the one* later! Or maybe you're like me and it's been two years since you've been ready. What if God is taking your match through something right now so they can be perfect for you a little later? That was the story of me and my wife. And we've been living for Jesus ever since.

Individual Devotional (15 Minutes)

1) Do you think dating someone that will tear you away from God is a viable option for believers?

2) Can you think of any friends who did get involved with someone who tore them away from Christ?

    a) If you could go back before they started dating, what would you say to them?

3) If you are single, do you believe God can bring the person of your dreams your way? How are you actively demonstrating faith that he can/will?

4) What are your overall thoughts on missionary or missional dating now?

5) Do you think because they say they are a Christian they really are by the way they live?

Couples Devotional (15 Minutes)

1) Had you ever heard the term missionary or missional dating before?

    a) What were your thoughts on it?

2) When it comes to being one with the father as Christ is with the father, what are somethings you as a couple can do together to draw closer to Christ?

3) Think about yourself individually, how can your girlfriend or boyfriend or person you're dating help encourage you in your relationship with Christ?

4) What are your thoughts on missionary or missional dating after this chapter? It's ok if you have differentiating thoughts.

Application

When it comes to not tearing each other further from our Heavenly Father we used this idea of someone with intent to tear you from your earthly father being the wrong person to date. Guys, this week reach out to her father, or stepfather and set up some time to get food or coffee and start building that connection. Girls, do the same with his mother or stepmom.

Chapter 6

"God's Timing"

[16] So the Jewish leaders began harassing Jesus for breaking the Sabbath rules. [17] But Jesus replied, "My Father is always working, and so am I." [18] So the Jewish leaders tried all the harder to find a way to kill him. For he not only broke the Sabbath, he called God his Father, thereby making himself equal with God. - John 5:17

Have you ever noticed God's timing is incredibly out of sync with your schedule and mental framework for when things should happen? Me too. It's like he doesn't get the memos or something? But have you ever wondered; what if you are in fact ready for the next chapter of your life, but your match made in heaven isn't?

That was certainly the case for me and my wife. It's funny to look back through my journals and see my lack of confidence in God. Like he wasn't working on it already, or didn't know what he was doing. Looking back to those darkest hours alone, I now see what Jesus was saying when he said "My father is always working." What I thought was apathy for his children's status on Facebook or a lack of faithfulness was quite the opposite. He was constantly tinkering in my life, refining all the imperfections my sinful nature and this fallen world had bestowed. Just as God is constantly working in your life right now as we speak! And if I could go back, I would encourage myself to take the focus off of me and place it on my future wife.

Oh, what I would give to go back for a brief second. I would tell him/me, every time I feel lonely, to pray for the loneliness my future wife felt. Every time I felt discouraged, to pray that the Holy Spirit would encourage her. All the times I doubted him, to reassure her that he is a good, good Father and his plans are beautiful. And if God needs you or me to wait a couple months, they are worth the wait! I would tell myself and you, if God wants you to wait a couple years, get excited! Because God had me and my wife wait twelve years before we ever noticed each other attending the exact same church!

I was twenty-three and she was nineteen years old. Those were the exact ages we meet. But funny enough we actually went to the same church for twelve years and God never gave us the opportunity to meet each other. Twelve years! Same church, not once! God actually moved heaven and hell just so we wouldn't find each other! That is until his approved time had come to pass.

Maybe you and your significant other are high school sweethearts. Or possibly junior high crushes. I'm jealous of you with everything in me.

I always wanted a story like that. Maybe you're a hopeless romantic like me. Which makes it a little crazy to think me and my wife essentially grew up right next to each other for twelve years and God never gave us the opportunity to encounter one another. Just like your future significant other might be right next to you as well. But God was always working, and knew what he was doing. We didn't meet for a reason during that time and a good reason too. We would have screwed it up.

You've already heard me confess, I was a prodigal indeed; a slow descent further and further from Christ until my dad's death which propelled me to rock bottom. I am so thankful my wife never met that Tyler, *old Tyler*, dead and gone Tyler. J.T. and Timberland got it right. And through the power of Jesus Christ's death and resurrection that old man is dead and the real me is here. And for all of those still single prodigals out there, you can probably relate. You're probably just as thankful that the person you're waiting for didn't see that brokenness. But what about all the devoted and committed Christ followers who have been faithful just about all their lives and are still single? How is that fair at all? Let me share a little of my wife's story now.

My wife grew up in an awesome Christian home that I'm blessed to be welcomed into. She has awesome Christ following parents. And she even possessed what we in Youth Ministry call the trifecta of faith: God fearing parents, a God fearing group of friends, and even God instilled morals. I'm just kidding; we don't have a name for that yet. Anyways, she had committed her life to Jesus from the time she was little and lived it out too. She was the Christ centered hottie who always went to small group, went to church on the weekends and even spent time with God. So when it came to being single all throughout high school and her entire life to be exact. When it came to all of the boys liking the girls who put-out instead of her; when it came to being single and unasked to her senior prom, she felt worthless.

She was crushed. She was committed to Christ. She was faithful always; she never strayed away in high school. Yet, God just seemingly sat back and let growing up in this cold world crush her.

In a perfect world I would have loved Jesus more than girls. I would have been more dedicated to him over football. I would have enjoyed his presence more than the party. But it's not a perfect world and when she needed me the most, God couldn't let her have me. I was a drunk with several addictions. I was a complete broken mess. A match made in heaven sure, but still currently going through hell. When she was following Christ and needed me to be there, I was nowhere to be found. And when I came back to church and was finally ready for her, she wasn't at church anymore.

So I guess the *coincidence* is when I did come to Christ, when he picked me up out of that ditch on the side of the road of life. When he washed my blood-stained clothes and made me new. She wasn't waiting for me any longer.

All the years my wife spent waiting on Christ, she seemingly had nothing to show for it. And that is exactly the angle the enemy used against her convictions. Where I made a slow decent into the ditch of brokenness, from middle school to twenty-one, my now wife took the shortcut. She went from child of God to prodigal son faster than you can say *college-lifestyle*. And when I had finally gotten to the place where I needed to be, and received the Father's approval to date, she wasn't there anymore, she was at clubs. And now I had to wait for God's timing, as she did all those years ago.

I wonder how many Christ followers out there believe the enemies lies. You know those small, sharp whispers like; *give in* to doubt, *give up* on faith, forget about your Heavenly Father and what Christ did, *it doesn't make a difference*. Looking back, as I would tell myself and tell my wife, I will encourage you too; don't give in, don't give up, don't believe the enemies lies. Your Heavenly Father is always working. It may be the sin in your life, or it may be a stronghold in theirs, rest assured he knows the plans he has for you. And whatever your situation is, no matter how painful, he will work those things together for good! Pray for your significant other you haven't met yet, they need it just as much as you do. And trust in your Father's approved timing. Keep surrendering your status to him and he will continue to move mountains for you. Slowly, steadily and surely, it will come to pass.

After several months of intense prodigal living, my wife had an immense Christ centered intervention. That's my wife though, a ball of energy always going a thousand miles an hour in whatever direction she chooses. And she did come back to Christ. She did come back to church and serving the body of Christ. Most of her breakthrough came from her aunt and uncle who provided some series counseling to her and so much more (thank you again for all that you did for my now wife. You gave me joy by blessing her). They invited her to stay with them on the other side of the U.S. and rehab from the *college-lifestyle*. And during her time out there, amongst the many things she learned, they instructed her to get plugged in, to get busy, and start serving in the church like crazy!

It's kind of crazy to see how Jesus really *is* always working. You see, old Peyton would serve at our church once or twice a month on the weekends with her family. But new Peyton, redeemed and restored Peyton, fleeing from temptation Peyton, started serving every week. Not just on the weekends, but throughout the work week too. And at a church our size, if she would have just served on the weekends, *we'd probably still haven't met yet*! She would be at Early Childhood's department, I would be at Middle School Ministry in a building on the other side of the church, and there would be thousands of other people at Cornerstone at any given time on the weekend to lose a face in. But the new Peyton, the Peyton who had to go through those hard times and end up on the other side of the country. The Peyton who would fly back restored and committed to Christ's calling over her life was the person serving her church several times a week. *And that is the only Peyton I could have met.* Because it was there at church, serving on a Tuesday night at 6:30pm that I first saw her. That is the Peyton I saw for the first time after twelve years at the same church. She is the match made in heaven God was *more than thrilled* to finally reveal. That is the Peyton who would stop me dead in my tracks across the campus, awestruck by this dark haired beauty. She is the woman of my dreams who had for the first time ever in her entire life, <u>surrendered every aspect of it to Jesus</u>. That is the Peyton who would captivate my heart and soul. She is the beauty I would chicken out three different times to go talk to. That is the Peyton who had the Father's approval, after much brokenness and healing, to find me. That is the Peyton who I would literally need confirmation from God almighty just to strengthen my resolve and introduce myself. She is my *Peyton with an E.*

Individual Devotional (15 Minutes)

1) What are some things timing-wise you wish God would pan out your way?

   a) How ok are you if he doesn't?

2) When it comes to the enemies lies, what are some of the doubts you wrestle with in your head?

3) How often do you pray for the person you're with or seeing right now, or your future spouse?

Couples Devotional (15 Minutes)

1) What do you think are some reasons God allowed us to get together when we did?

2) If God was and still is working all the things from your past together for good right now, what does that say about all the fights and problems that might happen in your relationship today? Is setting things right more important than being right in your arguments?

   a) Do you think God could work the junk in our lives together for good while we're together? Are we seeking forgiveness and reconciliation like we believe that?

3) What are some things you're currently waiting on God's timing for?

4) How have you seen God working in your current relationship?

   a) What might be some things hindering his Holy Spirit from working in your relationship right now?

Application
When it comes to waiting on God's timing for something, start a prayer journal together. Record all your prayers, write down the progress of those prayers, and at the end of this book see what God may have already done.

Chapter 7

"Confirmation... Or Simply a Response"

[34] "So don't worry about tomorrow, for tomorrow will bring its own worries. Today's trouble is enough for today. - Matthew 6:34
Also read 1 Samuel 14:1-17

As we finish up this section on the Father's approval and why it is so paramount to every aspect of life, including dating; it's my hopes to leave you less confused about the stigmas surrounding *Mr. or Mrs. Right*. I really do believe if you are surrendering your life to Christ (your entire life), then the Father's approval doesn't look like some Italian godfather you have to catch on his daughter's wedding day. It simply looks like getting your heart right with God before you try to involve another person's heart into your life and its mess. I've sat down with so many twenty-somethings who were just as perplexed and frustrated as I was when I started the Christian dating journey and trying to figure out who is *the one*. And amongst all of the overthinking and overanalyzing, I boiled it down to the simplest and least common denominators they needed to check before getting intentional about their potential relationship with that certain someone. I guess you can call it the lowest common denominator for Christian dating:

1. Are you extremely attracted to him or her?

2. Do they, or does it seem like they love the Lord their God with all of their heart, mind, soul, and strength?

That's it, the bottom floor, ground zero, lowest common denominator. So stop overthinking. If it's not meant to be it's not meant to be. If there's no chemistry trust me, you'll know it. If it's not meant to be, God will shut that door undeniably. Or slam it in your face. Don't overthink. If you're *not* attracted to that person in the least bit at all, is that really the person your Father would set you to spend the rest of your life with? <u>Is he a small God who can only coerce someone you can barely stand to suffer this life with, or is he the author of existence capable of</u>

doing exceedingly abundant above all our expectations!? Let's believe he is a good Father, and take it one step at a time. Don't be paralyzed about take-off before you ever step foot on the plane. Worry about first things first.

What did Jesus say? "Do not worry about tomorrow, for today has enough worries of its own." And I bet that frustrated the heck out of his disciples! When it came to long term planning, or planning ahead, or what the heck is going on this week, or what college should they go to, University or State? One of the only guarantees they ever really received about the future was *the son of man must die so he can rise again*, super practical Jesus. But despite the frustration, I bet they all learned what Jesus already knew, you can trust your Father to interact, to communicate, to come through and to guide your steps. He can respond and bring you confirmation and assurance. Don't overthink; he'll open or shut the doors in his own ways.

Don't overthink, just go for it. Ask them to coffee. Go on that coffee date, worst case scenario, she or he says they're not interested in a polite way and you get immediate closure, and immediately closer to your actual match made in heaven. Or you'll go out to coffee, proceed to a few dates after that and realize, there's nothing there, or they drive you nuts, or they belong in the looney bin. Trust me, without sex to complicate things, or the pursuit thereof; the writing will be on the walls like never before in your life! When you negate the *no pants dance* from the equation, it's simpler than 1 fish, 2 fish, 3… you get it.

I remember for me, God felt strangely far in between the time I first met someone I was attracted to and that first coffee date (don't worry; I'll layout that leap later). It was almost like clockwork. "Hey she's cute, I wonder if she might be the one…" Cue the strangely far feelings from God for the next few days. It's like he refused to coddle me with an approving answer until after I took that frightening leap of faith.

And it was frightening. Is she *the one* or is she not. The answer to that question has some long term implications, you know? "Should I talk to her, should I make a move, how can I know when it's cool from God? He is strangely far in this moment!" I could have really used someone to slap me in the face, sit me down, and layout the two least common denominators for proceeding to initiate conversation, and getting one step closer to finding out if God approves.

1. Are you extremely attracted to them?

2. Do they tangibly, visibly, undoubtedly love the Lord their God with all of their heart, mind, soul, and strength? Can you see any of this in their life?

Yes and yes? Good! Here's the cliff, go talk to them, and take the leap. And sure enough, after every leap of faith he provided confirmation in one way or another. <u>It's only when I didn't take the leap of faith that confirmation neither came nor did any idea of the Father's approval</u>.

So there she was, my match made in heaven, walking across the church campus back to her car like she's done two times in a row now as I gazed paralyzed in awe. Out of the twelve years that we had been attending the church at the same time, I had never seen here once. Yet the iron was hot, and so is she, it was time to strike. So I mustered up all the bravado and charm a 5'8", bald and bearded guy could muster and went off to make that dark haired beauty fall in love with this! Yet, I chickened out, again. I needed confirmation, and I knew the only way to get it was to put myself in the right position.

To my shame, I let this beautiful girl who stopped me dead in my tracks simply walk away more times than I could stand. And I wonder, how many of us get stuck on the cliffside of *what if*? I believe we need to get off of the sidelines of faith and into the game. Letting God do what he's supposed to do and decided the outcome. If you're looking for the Father's approval, take that leap of faith and trust in Christ and his ability to respond.

Think bold thoughts, "Their super attractive, they've been here six weeks now and they brought their Bible to church... I wonder if she'd be interested." Take some preemptive action when service gets out, and move into place. Contemplate the two least common denominators, take the leap of faith and see what happens. It can be pretty frightening, but that's what makes it exhilarating.

It's kind of scary to think that young men of faith used to need God's confirmation to attack an entire enemy army by themselves. Nowadays us guys can barely make the first move and talk to a single girl we think is cute in person. We have to poke them on Facebook. But I can't judge, I know I sure couldn't make the first move.

There I was, on the patio once again after a Saturday night service. Nothing out of the usual at church except my bearded self got invited up onstage to partake in a sermon illustration. I held up the card that said ENFJ, my pastor knows me well. And after scanning the sanctuary from up there, I didn't see my dark haired beauty in the crowd. "What was the point of coming to church tonight?" I thought. It's not as bad as it sounds I promise. Anyways, service was dismissed and I was out there on the patio, and behold, she *was* there that night, my match made in heaven. She must have been volunteering. And after service she was taking her usual path to the parking lot. Her sister was with her and they were b-lining it to the car. And after chickening out multiple times now, I grew pretty frustrated at myself. "Tonight's the night!" I thought. It was time for me to be man, sprint after her like Usain Bolt and totally come off as a bearded creep. Darn! There was no other possible way of talking to her than on the run, she was practically in a dead sprint every time I saw her after service. Fellowship hall my butt! As she was setting a personal record on her sprint time to the car, I gave up... I threw my hands up in the air with frustration; I took the gloves off, and threw up a sucker punch prayer! "God if you even love me, and if she is the one, **make her stop** so I can talk to her!" Two strides later she stops dead in her dash. She turns, hands her volunteer name badge to her sister. And her sister walks back from whence they came. Peyton then proceeds to sit down at a nearby table. I can't recall if anyone saw me or not, but at that moment I'm pretty sure I did the Tim Tebow!

Shout out to God with a voice of triumph! I'm ecstatic; I can't believe what just happened! Who needs bravado when you got God almighty in your corner? I walk up, do what normal people do, and introduce myself by my first and last name. Wait normal people don't do that. But, BOOM! We hit it off. She's a total spas just like me. Her sister came back and joined the conversation, and we chatted for forty-five minutes while the facility team was trying to lock down the campus!

"I can't believe our conversation is going so good!" I thought. I can't believe I'm finally talking to her. I can't believe she actually sat down after my lame excuse of a prayer. But I think that's how it works when it comes to seeing God respond. You give it up to God and his approval, make the move and take the leap, he'll control the outcome. Our Father loves when his children trust him with their lives and the smallest details thereof. Of course he will open the right doors for you and of course he will close the wrong ones. And if you are earnest in doing his will, he'll open up the doors, provide all the confirmation you need, and even sugar coat it with some unexplainable *coincidences* for you!

When it comes to the Father's approval, I trust he'll let us know. He's not an absent Father in our lives, he's a present Father, a good Father. It won't be shrouded in mystery for years, there will be a spark, or chemistry, or he'll even cause the fastest girl at church to literally stop in her tracks, turn to her sister and hand over her name badge for her sister to take back to the Early Childhood room by herself, while she unexplainably sits down for no reason at all. Casually after some poor sucker twenty meters behind couldn't catch up and threw up some poor prayer in desperation, "Lord if she's the one make her stop so we can talk."

And if you're not convinced God can bring purpose to every millimeter of your life if you give it to him. Check this out. The same Saturday night that I had talked to Peyton for the first time, was actually the same Saturday night that her family had ever noticed me for the first time when I was helping out on stage for the sermon illustration. So as Peyton and her sister, Ashlyn, walk through the front door, and the first thing Ashlyn said was, "Duck dynasty asked out Peyton." Their mom and dad knew exactly what that meant and who I was.

Here's where things get weird. They knew exactly who Ashlyn was referring to because when I went up on stage and her dad saw me up there for the first time ever, he had a quick thought in his head where he envisioned me and Peyton being together. But it was just a random thought that passed quickly. Yet, their mom had a completely similar thought about the same thing. She had a thought of me and Peyton getting together, dating! Once again it was just a quick thought though, quickly come, quickly go. That is until Ashlyn mentioned my coffee date proposal when her dad revealed the thought that came to his head and her mom revealed that was exactly what she had envisioned too! They all were pretty confounded. The almost exact same thought, thought completely separately yet at the exact same time by two different people, talk about confirmation!

But that's our Father for you. Those types of big and little God inspired accounts and stories in scripture. That's our God who never changes. Who moved powerfully back then and moves in power and awe now and will never ever not move in power and glory. And he wants you to experience a relationship with him. A supernatural connection between creator and creation! And when you've surrendered your life and your dating journey to him he'll move mountains to reveal your path if you let him. Just like he did for me and Peyton that night, one of the most important nights of my life.

Oh and if your think Peyton said yes to my coffee date proposal after we talked and had an incredible spark-igniting conversation for forty-five minutes, you'd be wrong. She said maybe... MAYBE! But we'll talk about that in our next section, *Intentional*.

Individual Devotional (15 Minutes)

1) Do you, or did you think God could and would be able to bring you someone you're incredibly attracted to and loves him as much or more than you do?

2) How have you tended to overthink or over complicate things when dating in the past?

3) What are some leaps of faith you overthought and never took?

Couples Devotional (15 Minutes)

1) What are some of the different ways you've seen God confirm or deny certain paths in your life?

2) What might be some next steps in your relationship that God might be opening doors for?

3) What are some areas he's challenging you to wait and is keeping the door closed on?

Application

What is the next step in your relationship? Take some time today and have that conversation about why it might be the right time, or why it might not be.

A Transition

Chapter 8

Girlfriends Don't Exist

I stood there with my old friend, defeat in his eyes. He spilled his sentences and emotions out one after another. But one of his sentences could not have been phrased more perfectly, "I don't know how I should treat her! I'm giving her all the love the Bible says a husband should give his wife! But she keeps treating me like crap!" This definitely created some questions considering the fact they weren't married yet... Still, he brought up a good point.

As different as my friend's situation might be from yours (or similar who knows), how many of us can relate to his confusion? How many of us have no idea what the biblical mandates are for picking up chicks at the mall, or the right amount of time scripturally to text or call after you get their number? Or how do I display the correct amount of affection in correlation to the number of dates we've been on in a biblical way. Or what about the more fun questions like; how am I supposed to treat my boyfriend when our relationship is coming to an end, but I don't want it to? Or this started out as a booty call, but I just gave my life to Jesus, now what? What about the old, he likes me, and I like him, now what?

There is definitely a lack of clarity here in the Bible when it comes to dating because back in the biblical era there was no dating. And as an old pastor once told me "She's either your sister in Jesus or your wife, there's nothing in between." As helpful advice as this was trying to lose my prodigal lust (which definitely helped since I didn't want to be awkward and commit incest in God's eyes); it didn't help my dating questions. And it actually wasn't biblically rooted either.

In the Bible there are three primary New Testament instances of a man's relationship to a woman he isn't related to. She is number one, your sister in Christ, number two, your wife in Christ, or number three, and what most old Christian adages miss, *your fiancée*! And I believe this often overlooked process of Jewish engagement as found in scripture provides some helpful ideas, markers and steps to go from so-called *siblings* in Christ, to getting married (which yes sounds immensely creepy as I write it on paper). Here are some ideas and steps that we all need today.

For me, I knew how to *get girls* as a prodigal, but I knew finding *the one* and dating her couldn't be the same as what I used to do in regards to the kingdom of heaven. And no matter what your background is; prodigal, perfect child, or pastor's kid, Christian dating can seem more confusing and have more twists and turns than a Rubix Cube! So check out these Jewish customs of engagement and marriage that really helped bring me context and a greater understanding for how to go about finding, courting, dating, and treating my future *Mrs.*

Here are some of those steps according to the Jewish customs of engagement and marriage in a brief description that our time will allow. Feel free to do more research on your own if you like. The first step is;

1. Shiddukhim - Preliminary arrangements to the legal betrothal usually done *by the father* to select the bride for his son.

During this time of the father selecting a bride for his son, the father could appoint a Shadkhan also known as a **matchmaker**. Just like Abraham appointed Eleazer to find a wife for his son Isaac. Just like the Holy Spirit convicts us of our sins, and brings us to the *son* and his forgiveness. What did Jesus say? "For my Father has given them to me." In regards to who comes and finds faith in his son, our *Heavenly Father* is the one to select them, through the Holy Spirit's work in us.

2. Ketubah - "Written" - The written contract of marriage **declaring the intentions** and transparent, upfront expectations of the union.

This is where the groom promises to support his bride on a legal document, something we still sort of do today with a marriage license. Also on the document the bride would stipulate her dowry or financial status. And even though I haven't heard this referenced by others, I'm pretty sure it's safe to say that the Bible is like our "Ketubah," declaring the intentions and transparent, upfront expectations between us, and our heavenly bridegroom Jesus, for here on earth into eternity.

3. <u>Mohar</u> - "The bridal price" - The payment by the groom to the bride's family. This payment would ultimately **change her status** once paid and set her free from her parent's household.

Just as Jesus was the ransom to set us free from where we once belonged; the house of sin and death. Now after his payment, his ransom and sacrifice, we have been set free from the family of sin and shame and our status is now counted a child of God.

4. <u>Mikveh</u> - "Ritual immersion" - To prepare for the betrothal, it was common for the bride and groom to separately take a ritual immersion.

Just as Jesus did first by John the Baptist to fulfill all righteousness. Then Jesus commissioned us to be baptized and baptize others as well. Ritual immersion taken separately for our union.

5. <u>Eyrusion</u> - "Betrothal or kiddushim" - Set apart/sanctified. A time when the couple is **set apart** to prepare themselves for the covenant of marriage.

In regards to the different aspects of betrothal, there would first be an exchanging of gifts, the *Matan*. Its purpose was to be a reminder to his bride during their days of separation of his love for her, a reminder that he was thinking of her and that he would return to receive her as his wife. We kind of do the same today with the engagement ring. Which reminds me of what Paul said in 2 Corinthians 1:22 "And who (God) has also put his seal on us and given us his Holy Spirit in our hearts as a guarantee." Jesus places the gift of his spirit like a seal on us as a guarantee that we belong to him. And after this step, the groom would then go and prepare a home and a place for them to consummate their marriage on his father's property. What did Jesus say before the ascension, "I'm going to go prepare a place for you in my Father's house?"

There are some more pretty incredible steps and parallels in this process that we don't have time for today. But it's my hope that we would all start to see Jesus in these Old Testament rituals. My wish is that we would begin to realize how perfectly stitched together the tapestry of human history is with Jesus as the scarlet thread, woven throughout all of existence. It is my prayer that we would begin to see these specific Old Testament rituals as they truly are, clear indications of how Jesus loves us; like a bridegroom waiting for his bride. If nothing is gained from this chapter about Christian dating, I can live with that as long as you just catch a mere glimpse of how passionately, intrinsically involved Jesus is to you, like a groom to his bride!

But when it comes to Christian dating and courting, hopefully this brings some clarity too. Notice one of the first steps in ancient Jewish engagement and marriage involves a matchmaker. As all of my single Christian friends would agree, blessed be the matchmakers, for theirs is the kingdom of heaven! If you don't know any cute single Christians out there, you're going to need a matchmaker. Just like Abraham sent out Eleazer to find a bride for his son, you're going to need someone to set you up with your next potential wifey or hubby. This Old Testament story being an analogy for the way the our Heavenly Father sends out the Holy Spirit, the advocate and *helper* to convict the world of its sin and draw people to his son, Jesus Christ. How fitting that the name Eleazar just so coincidently means, *God is helper*. And help I did have, too much sometimes. So many blind dates that never seemed to pan out into a second date, ever. That definitely wasn't fun considering I'd try to be intentional and communicate how I felt. Even if I felt nothing for them in the least bit at all whatsoever and never in a million years would ever feel anything here on earth or kingdom come. This takes us to the next crucial step in *how to date*.

The *Ketubah*, a written contract declaring clear expectations and intentions; this is the part where a marriage contract was drawn up. Hopefully your first date doesn't involve a marriage contract, but it will involve being intentional and being upfront if you're going to have a second date. If you're interested in them and would like a second date, tell them. However, as a Christ follower, I dare say that you would also have to be intentional and tell them if you're uninterested. Not just *I'll call you*, and then never do. That's what unbelievers do, and I'm almost certain Jesus calls us to be more empathetic than that. Being transparent and upfront is something you're going to have to do throughout dating. You might not be setting up clear expectations for a union, but you will be laying out clear expectations for a relationship. We'll talk more on being intentional in Section 2.

This takes us to the third step, changing her status or the *Mohor*, the bridal price. Once the groom paid this amount to the bride's family, this would change her status and she would ultimately be set free from her parents' house to be with him. And even if it's just on Facebook, as a couple you're going to have to make it official and change your status from just dating or seeing each other, to *in a relationship*. I can't think of any successful relationships that don't even amount to this change. And it might be a strange ritual to us today like the *Mikveh* is, but how can you traverse all the obstacles being in a relationship in today's day and age will throw at you if you can't even be upfront and honest about changing your status, making it official and taking yourself *off the market*, being set apart? This takes me to our next step.

Eyrusion was a time to be set apart, betrothal or kiddushim. It was a time for the couple to be set apart and prepare themselves for the covenant of marriage. And even though they were literally set apart for a period of time, before meeting back up together, we are to be off the market and set apart from others, exclusive with each other being in a relationship. <u>And this time of being set apart from the single life, in a relationship, is preparation for marriage</u>. You get to know each other's habits, characteristics and idiosyncrasies. You get past the honeymoon stage and take off the rose colored glasses. You share experiences and bond. You fight, and fight again, then finally work through it, and bond even closer. And if he or she's the one, you'll figure it out. And if you do it God's way, he'll sustain it.

I know this helped me before I met Peyton. It laid out some markers for me to go by, unlike my friend who treated every girl he was dating like his wife in all the wrong ways. I heard this analogy of Jewish engagement and Jesus from one of my favorite communicators and it blew me away. I had to research it and read it for myself. It changed how I saw God, it astounded me how passionately he loves us, the church, his bride. And to simply show off it seems, Jesus wove himself and his relationship to us in the Old Testament throughout the process of Hebrew marriage. Look it up yourself and see. It reminds me of all the times I show off to my love, just to make her smile and know how crazy I am for her.

Individual Devotional (15 Minutes)

1) What have been some of your questions when it comes to dating and Christianity today?

2) Can you identify any of those steps or markers as things you would do or have done?

3) How does this symbolism in the ancient Jewish engagement and marriage process speak to you about God's passion for you?

Couples Devotional (15 Minutes)

1) What have been some of your questions when it comes to dating and Christianity today?

2) What are some of the road bumps and issues you're running into dating in a Christian way?

3) Are there any of these steps we may have overlooked or not utilized? Are they any steps we may need to take?

Application
Go throughout the Bible and find one example for some of these steps. Talk about what you found, and compare how they used to end up getting hitched to how we do things today.

Section 2 Overview

Intentionality

[25] "Was it to me you were bringing sacrifices and offerings during
the forty years in the wilderness, Israel?" - Amos 5:25
Also read 2 Kings 17:15 (NIV) / 2 Kings 17:40-41 (NIV)

Intentionality truly is a lost art. Intentionality is the catalyst to dating in a purposeful, Christ centered way. Heck, Intentionality is the catalyst to *living* in a purposeful, Christ centered way. I don't know too many Christians who accidentally lived their purpose or calling out year after year, stumbling into greater impact every following year. Do you? Probably not, and being intentional when it comes to dating can be just as foreign here in America.

Dating is a jungle and intentionality is the map. And just like the Indiana Jones movies, you're going to be in a world of hurt, and have an immensely frustrated woman on your hands if you let everything go array with no direction guys. The bad news is that even in the best of relationships, she'll occasionally want to give you a dramatic slap, just like the ones Doctor Jones is accustomed to. But the good news is with a little intentionality you can push back that frustration melting point into the safe confines of a secure relationship, instead of an immediate explosion in the beginning when things are still fragile. Here's what I mean.

Let's go back to the jungle imagery. It's safe to say, dating is a thick jungle. It's rough terrain, there's danger around every corner and you're sure to feel lost before getting through it in one piece. To navigate this jungle and get to the altar together you'll need intentionality. It's the map.

Remember my friend Chris from Chapter 3? Without being intentional about his feelings, his desires and his convictions; he stumbled from chatting, to flirting, to playful touching, all the way to making a mistake one night that cost him immensely. They were not intentional when it came to how they felt about each other and wandered into a life altering moment that cost him dearly.

Even with being intentional, my wife and I still managed to barely escape the dating season and get to the altar unscathed. How often do we know the right path, the right thing we need to do, the right way to do something, or how things *should* happen, yet somehow as human beings we *don't* do it. Being intentional is a necessity. We so often end up lost in our decisions, what we should or should not do. How we feel or don't feel. What we think and what we desire. Keeping intentionality at the forefront of your relationship will help navigate all those things on the inside that always tend to take your relationship to the next level of complicated.

Intentionality is the map. We go from here to there and there to that. We go from A to B to C all the way to Z. We go from establishing communication, to an easy *pre-date* environment like coffee, followed up with the invitation to a real date. And if things go well there, proceed to a second date, third date and forth date. And after establishing a base-camp of *dating*, have an intentional conversation of how we feel about each other and where we see this going. Which is one of two directions by the way. In a Facebook official relationship or friend-zone. Nothing in between, that's the *Netflix and chill* zone. And once you get past the jungle pitfalls of dating, that's where we utilize our purpose as Christ followers as a vehicle for which we can begin to experience satisfaction and fulfillment even without sex yet.

As dangerous as jungles can be, not all jungles have forests or rain. Just ask the recently released Israelites from Egyptian slavery. They wandered for forty years. Not because they were lost geographically, but because they were lost spiritually. In the book of Amos, God makes it quite clear where the hearts of the Jewish people have belonged for all those hundreds of years. And God doesn't pull any punches. "Was it to me you were bringing sacrifices and offerings during the forty years in the wilderness, Israel?" They actually belonged to the foreign gods. The idols the other nations worshiped. The ancient Israelites didn't wander the desert because they were geographically lost, they wandered because they were spiritually lost. Their spiritual compass got mixed up between what feels good and *who* is good (Mark 10:18), and the worship thereof. And it took an entire generation to pass away before God was able to raise-up a generation of people with more *intentional* faith in him. As you, a child of God, try to come out of the Egypt of dating (the way the world dates) and head to the promised land of an abundant life together, you will need to be intentional from the start if you are to navigate the wilderness in less than forty years, or survive it.

Even though intentionality in dating is the difference between a pleasant experience and those painful horror stories you hear from your friends or the internet, you will need two things to follow that map. You'll need courage and vulnerability. Yes, men, you will need to have courage believe it or not. And women, as painful as it can be from life's past wounds, you'll need to become vulnerable once again. Like Indiana Jones, men, we'll need the machete of courage to cut through the brush of ambiguousness, confusion, assumptions, and false pretenses so we can clear a path for girls to be vulnerable; allowing them to take the next step forward in their feelings, emotions and trust. If we don't clear away the confusion and put ourselves out there with courage as men, can we really expect them to be vulnerable with us as women? If we don't clear out the assumptions and make the first move can we really expect women to climb the walls of insecurity life has forced them to build and lock themselves in like the imagery of Rapunzel in her tower? Well, the answer is yes sometimes, and in some cases girls have learned who they've needed to adapt to be by the scars of this life. But very rarely will a man's spirit follow an overwhelming bravado of a woman without developing insecurities of his own.

Courage and Vulnerability. All I'm saying is if you do believe scripture that men and women are actually different. And both are created in the image of God, but with different aspects imbued in them. Then those aspects complement one another, not tear each other down, or subject one under the other. So with those different qualities in mind, men, it's time to "Be strong and courageous" as God told Joshua. And women, when you find a man who will do this for you and be intentional about how he feels, you will have to overcome the insecurities, lies and whispers of the enemy that have been towering over you from when you were still a child.

As we dive into being intentional and the different steps thereof, keep these undertones in your heart. Courage and vulnerability. I've never met any man who lives an abundant life without bravery. The type of bravery that can be intentional and upfront with their feelings. And I've never met any woman who lives a life overflowing with joy, without letting her guard down once in a while and letting vulnerability occur.

So let's dive into this dance of dating, and check out some steps.

Individual Devotional (15 Minutes)

1) How are you being intentional about surrendering your life to Christ?

   a) Or does your relationship with Christ feel more like a religion?

2) Where have your past flings derailed from not being intentional?

   a) How does that indicate the importance of staying intentional in this relationship or your future one if single?

3) Is courage or vulnerability a strong point of yours when it comes to be intentional and putting yourself out there?

Couples Devotional (15 Minutes)

1) Are you being intentional about putting Christ first in your relationship? Or is he somewhere on the sidelines?

2) Is your relationship headed anywhere or are you just dating to date?

   a) Is finding someone to spend the rest of your life with isn't the direction it's heading, why might you still be together?

3) What are some areas of your life you need to start being intentionally open and transparent about? Instead of keeping them sealed and acting out of insecurities about.

4) Where is intentionality lacking in your relationship?

Application

In those areas you did write down about being more intentionally open and transparent, each of you reach out to an individual person that you can be intentional and open with outside of your relationship with as well. Ask them to keep you accountable and to check in from time to time.

Chapter 9

Males Take the Lead

[1] Therefore, since we are surrounded by such a huge crowd of
witnesses to the life of faith, let us strip off every weight that slows us
down, especially the sin that so easily trips us up. And let us run with
endurance the race God has set before us. [2] We do this by keeping our
eyes on Jesus, the champion *who initiates* and perfects our faith. Because
of the joy awaiting him, he endured the cross, disregarding its shame.
Now he is seated in the place of honor beside God's throne.
- Hebrews 12:1-2

I'll never forget second grade. Actually, I've forgotten almost all of
second grade. But one portion will always stick. Square dancing! My
second grade teacher used to take time out of our afternoons and
dedicate it to teaching us how to square dance. How she got second
graders to do this blows my mind! But she did! She probably moonlights
as a cat-herder.

Square dancing was hard. Remembering the steps were easy
enough, but dancing with the girls, check that, *square* dancing with the
girls was immensely hard on a second grade boy. Holding hands with a
girl, moving with the rhythm, executing fast paced steps in overalls; I
don't know how I did it. And perhaps the hardest part about square
dancing in second grade was *taking the lead*.

It reminds me a lot of choosing to be intentional. Last chapter we
introduced the idea of guys going first, paving the way with courage
down the relational pathway allowing girls to be vulnerable. And when it
comes to paving the way and being intentional, that means you're going
to take the lead guys. With things like introductions and initiating
conversation, with things like asking her to coffee, or asking her out on
that first date, and even explaining how you feel about her and so on.
Being intentional means we take the lead, just as Christ took the lead and
initiated our faith.

When God stopped my wife dead sprint to the car after that
Saturday night service and she actually sat down, I was stoked! She was
actually approachable for once. And I introduced myself and initiated the

conversation. We chatted for almost an hour about everything it seemed. But amongst our laughing and learning more about one another, the lessons learned from second grade remained in the back of my head. I'm going to have to take the lead and invite her to take the *next step* with me, coffee.

So as the facility crew began herding us off campus to close it down, I took that first next step. As the anticipation grew in my head and the moment was paramount, I knew it was now or never. And I said, "Hey, if you're not busy next week, would you like to go grab a cup of coffee with me some time?" "Boom, nailed it, first try, ya boy is on fire tonight!" I thought. The bow and curtsy of our conversation flowed into the perfect next step! And away we went. Except for the fact that she didn't say yes, or yeah, or even sure... She said **maybe**! "Are you freaking kidding me!? Maybe!? I'm your match made in heaven girl!" I thought to myself. "I just saw God stop you're eager-to-get-home butt and sit it down on this bench so I can simply approach you without coming off too creepy! And you say maybe?" My head was racing with a million thoughts like this at once. And after one second and a million thoughts through my head later, she said "Maybe" again, and was back to the races.

Faux pas! Miss-step! How did I read that situation wrong!? How could she be disinterested!? I am her match made in heaven (granted I did have a beard down to my chest at this point)! We clicked for forty-five minutes. The chemistry was explosive! Yet, maybe?

And unfortunately, this is the risk we run being strong and courageous. It's our role to take these scary first steps as men. But I really do believe God loves it when his children make brave moves in this life aligned with the beat of his word and the rhythms of his grace. Bold leaps of faith that give him control of the outcome.

God loves it when men take the lead. Think about it. God is an *initiator*. Before the beginning, God *spoke*. When man was just lying there, a lifeless corpse from the dust, God *breathed*. When mankind first sinned in the garden, God *came* walking in the cool of the day to us. When the world needed to rebirth and to be cleansed by water, God *warned* Noah. When creation lost touch with its creator, God *called* Abraham. When God's people were enslaved in Egypt, God *chose* Moses. When the Israelites couldn't make their way home, God *lead* them by a pillar of smoke in the day and by fire at night. And after centuries and millennia of taking the lead, and letting the nations of the earth "Seek after God and perhaps feel their way toward him and find him" (Acts 17:27), he *sent* his one and only son that whosoever would believe in him would not perish, but have everlasting life. From before the beginning, God initiated, Jesus took the lead, the Holy Spirit moved. And call it spiritual DNA I guess, God loves it when we initiate and meet a need, heal a hurt, right a wrong, forgive a person, take the lead, or simply step up and step into the calling on our lives. I believe he honors it.

You see, Peyton said maybe because she didn't know me well enough in her mind. Even though I still to this day believe a forty-five minute, chemistry filled conversations took care of that need, she didn't. I had taken that leap of faith, I made the first move, and apparently I had leaped to my death. But God has a way of bringing the dead back to life. And he did something completely incredible in this predicament when I was completely incapable of anything in my own strength.

That night I was in all of Peyton's dreams. Every single one of them. And then the next night I was in every single one of Peyton's dreams again. And while I was sulking and licking my wounds in retreat, God was advancing our future relationship. She continued to dream about me every night in a row for *two whole weeks*! Talk about confirmation.

After bumping into each other the next few weeks at church (she was actually looking for me now), I left a note on her car. Don't judge me; I was ready to try anything. And she finally agreed to coffee. I mean, she might as well spend a little time with me in reality considering the fact that she was spending every sleeping moment hanging out with me in her dreams. So we set a time and place. Starbucks of course.

And coffee went great! It went amazing! We spent three and a half hours just talking. And something happened that never happened to me before in any previous relationship, or on any date. A complete stranger walked up to us and said we are a great couple, and are so good for each other! Confirmation after confirmation. I never felt so enthralled and at peace at the same time before.

But even in the midst of our effortless conversation, I knew it was on me to be intentional and take the next step first. And sure enough after three and a half hours our conversation was coming to a close. I asked her if she would like to get sushi with me next week. As I cringed my teeth in anticipation hoping that this time over three hours was enough time for her to get to know a guy, she said yes. The first time!

And after the second, third and fourth date, I always kept the same routine. Ending our time together by being intentional and inviting her to our next date together or setting up plans. Never keeping her guessing about what comes next or how I felt about her. I took the lead.

We went step by step, one after the other to the rhythm of our scheduling and unconfined excitement. It was a ball to pursue someone with the Father's approval. And taking the lead prevented any mishaps in communication or clarity. We simply glided like one, two, three, one, two, three.

I truly believe taking the lead is something we as potential future hubby's have to do. Jesus always did/does this for us, his bride. Starting with baptism. He modeled this for us to fulfill all righteousness. And now we follow. He pointed people to the Father, now we follow. He laid down his life for the church, and now we are to pick up our cross and you guessed it, follow. Step by step, to the beautiful rhythms of grace. Men, we are to take the lead so women can take the ever harder step of opening up and be vulnerable once again.

Individual Devotional (15 Minutes)

1) How has taking the lead and making the first move failed you before?

    a) Do you think that past experience might still be affecting you today?

2) When is the last time you took a leap of faith and gave God complete control of the outcome?

3) How can you begin to take the lead in other aspects of your life in Christ, like forgiving someone, joining a ministry to serve in, etc.?

Couples Devotional (15 Minutes)

1) Is there an intentional conversation you might be holding back from in your time together?

    a) Is there any clarity you need to intentionally ask about or talk about right now?

2) How can God honor and bless your relationship if you start to be more intentional about keeping it founded on him?

3) What are some of the distractions that have kept you from living more intentionally focused on Christ?

Application

On a piece of paper write draw a line down the middle. On the left, write down all the different ways you are and can start keeping your relationship founded on Christ. On the right, write down all of the things that are distracting you from living more focused on Christ. Add this to your prayer journal, and keep checking weekly on how you're doing.

Chapter 10

D.T.R.

[13] Therefore, put on every piece of God's armor so you will be able to resist the enemy in the time of evil. Then after the battle you will still be standing firm. [14] Stand your ground, putting on the belt of truth and the body armor of God's righteousness. - Ephesians 6:13-14

Defining the relationship. When it comes to the lack of intentionality in dating today, even society has encapsulated a cure, *defining the relationship*. And if this broken world has recognized a need to be intentional while dating; the same world which has had *professional psychologist* also recommend adultery as a tool for marital improvement, how much more do we as Christ followers need to recognize the need to be open, and honest? How much more should we recognize the importance of being intentional and defining the relationship?

Defining the relationship is a paramount step when it comes to intentionally dating in a Christ honoring way. Defining the relationship brings clarity, and communication and assurance. It's what enables and protects trust and vulnerability. If dating is a jungle and intentionality is the map, then D.T.R. helps us navigate through all of the anxiety and worry we experience from the *what if's*? The "What if they're not feeling this like I'm feeling this?" Or the, "What if he keeps dragging me along just to use me?" Or even the, "What if she's just playing me like she's playing some other guys?" D.T.R. helps navigate through the infinite possibilities of *what if* our mental constructs can compose.

Looking back, this is one area that we didn't struggle in. Being two prodigals, we were going to make it quite clear that no one comes before our first relationship with Jesus this time. I remember sitting at that Starbucks for the first time together and she flat out said, "I only date if it's going to lead to something. I don't date just to date." Now that might take some people back, but I was enthralled. And all I had to say in response was "I agree." And from there, things like being intentional and D.T.R. were no problem.

We started on the right foot. Being upfront. Which made each following and harder conversation that much easier. Unlike all those other relationships we as people can find ourselves in, where we spend so much time together yet never actually *go there* in our conversation. Thus never actually going anywhere *relationally*.

We set clear expectations on the front end. Negotiated terms if you like. Out of the three and a half hours of laughing and enjoying ourselves, maybe five minutes were dedicated to being intentional and defining some particulars about *if* this is ever going to turn into something. Particulars like doing it God's way. We've done it the world's way, and we've done it our way, but it never actually went the way we'd hope for in the end. Particulars like praying before we make it official, always leaving room for God to give us confirmation, or split us up, never leaving it to what we think is best. Kind of crazy huh?

And crazy it very well might be, especially if intentionality has never been a part of the dating process for you. But perhaps this lack of intentionality is the exact driver to the frustrations and let downs in your prior romances, *or things*, since you never really made it official. <u>This could be the fixed point where the relationships you've been in differ and become the relationship you actually want</u>.

Intentionality, defining the relationship, these things provide transparency, honesty, and truth. They enable you up front, from the very beginning to start building this relationship on a solid foundation. Much unlike the uneasy, unsteady, unsure, ready-to-fall flings and relationships we've been in before. It's through intentionality and defining the relationship each step of the way that you proactively lay brink after healthy brick of conversation on a solid foundation that can last your whole life. What did Jesus say about building on a solid foundation? <u>And these two things are not only crucial for being relationally proactive, but for relational protection as well</u>.

Defining the relationship protects your potential relationship like nothing else. Truthful conversations like this remind me of what Ephesians six describes as *the belt of truth*. In this section of Ephesians six, Paul is describing some essentials we as Christ followers need to utilize if we're going to make it off of this rock and into the next life in one piece. Including if we are to stand firm *after the battle*, or battles this life throws at us. He likens Roman armor and weaponry to the spiritual realities we use defensively and offensively against the enemy of our soul and the hordes of hell trying to tear us apart from Christ.

Each individual item is crucial sure. But most military historians will tell you the Roman belt was the most pertinent and dynamic item the soldier needed. For starters, it kept the entire ensemble together, allowing him to do and utilize what he needed in each situation. Next, it was his primary source of protection in close combat. This wasn't a D&G fashion piece, it was an immensely thick and wide, sturdy set of leather protecting his abdominals. The most common point of attack in ancient days. It protected the commonly attacked place, their core.

What about for us today? With the imagery above in mind, Paul likens truth to the protection of our most vulnerable and attacked places. And amongst all the vital parts of life in faith, perhaps one of the most attacked facets of life is our Christ honoring relationships. Think about it, Satan has been causing division in relationships since *the garden*! And if dating is a jungle, then Christian dating is like Vietnam, constantly ambushed by enemy assault. And when we as Christ followers put on the belt of truth and have these honest and defining conversations about how we feel and what our intentions are moving forward, we protect and ensure our potential relationship from the constant bombardment of the enemy's lies.

That's what Peyton and I experienced personally. Being intentional during or after each date about how we truly feel. What we thought God was saying, or what he's doing, opening or closing doors, laying out our expectations. All of which can be scary to admit conversationally. But the apostle Paul doesn't tell us to put the belt of truth on for good measure, or so we can be good little boys and girls in Christ. He tells us to put on the belt of truth so we can actually get up and stand to our feet during the *time of evil* and *after the battle*, even when everything else around us might be scorched earth. Even with circumstances burning down around us, being intentional can keep our relationship standing!

Individual Devotional (15 Minutes)

1) When it comes to defining the relationship, how is your track record? Is this something you're intentional about, or is it just something you don't pay too much attention to.

2) How can defining the relationship or having these upfront conversations be a scary aspect of the dating process to you?

3) How are you when it comes to the *belt of truth*? Are painfully truthful conversations something you run from?

Couples Devotional (15 Minutes)

1) Have you defined the relationship yet? What is stopping you?

2) What are some *what if's* you thought before that defining the relationship will help eliminate? Or did help eliminate?

3) Besides D.T.R., how are we doing when it comes to being intentional and upfront with one another?

   a) Is there anything you can share right now?

4) What are some of your expectations in and about this relationship?

Application
In your prayer journal, talk about, then write down those different expectations you have for this relationship and pray for Christ to continually help you meet these. Constantly come back to that list throughout this book and see how you're doing.

Chapter 11

Dating For the Hell of It

[24] Don't you realize that in a race everyone runs, but only one person gets the prize? So run to win! [25] All athletes are disciplined in their training. They do it to win a prize that will fade away, but we do it for an eternal prize. [26] So I run with purpose in every step. I am not just shadowboxing. [27] I discipline my body like an athlete, training it to do what it should. Otherwise, I fear that after preaching to others I myself might be disqualified. -1 Corinthians 9:24-27
Also read Hebrews 12:1-4 / Isaiah 40:31 / Philippians 3:13-14 /
2 Timothy 4:7-9

Have you ever noticed the Bible talks a lot about *running the race*? If you haven't read most of the New Testament trust me, it talks about running enough to make you feel guilty for the donut you indulged on in the break room earlier this week. And our friend Paul mentions something that immensely resonated with me in 2 Cor. 9 when he said "I don't run aimlessly."

It resonated with me because I used to play football in high school and college. I even ran track a little too. Both have an end zone or a finish line, an end point to run to. But it also resonated with me because it reminded me of how I used to approach dating, *aimlessly*.

I would fall for a girl over here, or I would start talking to a girl over there. Some girl, somewhere. Whichever opportunity presented itself. Or perhaps the worst part about dating is when you end up together *again* with someone you just ended it with months earlier. How does that happen? How did I end up back in that situation again? And the truth of the matter is that I didn't really know, I just did somehow. And I went around that doomed track of disaster one more time, *again*.

How often does this happen in your life or perhaps a friend's life you can think of? You know, that one couple who broke things off again last month, but showed up to the surprise party together? Or that one couple who always manages to have a World War II sized blow up in public again, no matter where they go? Or how about that one friend who always takes back their ex again after the one millionth time of breaking up? How did that happen, *again*? Or let's get a little more specific, what about that person you can't help but want to (or really do) text late at night when loneliness creeps up and you feel more alone than ever before... How did you get there again after saying you wouldn't a thousand times before? How do we keep ending up *there* in such toxic situations, or relationships, or moments, or even one night stands? It's because we not aiming for anything else, we in our dating lives are aimless.

I know this resonates with *old Tyler*. And it drove me crazy, "How did I end up here again?" I would think. It was like my life was stuck on a bad loop. It was like I was running with all my energy, depleting my life dry, but getting nowhere! It was like I was on the worst invention ever made, **a treadmill**. Just running aimlessly, but never actually getting anywhere. Never actually making any progress in my life. Can you relate when it comes to your dating experience, or maybe in the lives of those around you?

Maybe that's why God chooses to use so much imagery around *running*. Perhaps that's why Paul challenges believers to step off the proverbial treadmill of life and invites us towards a purpose, towards a goal, towards a meaningful existence in this life. Meaningfulness in every aspect of it! Staying disciplined, least we disqualifies ourselves from all the progress we've strived for.

And it's verses like these that set the tone for mine and Peyton's dating life. It's verses like these that laced up our cleats of intentionality and clear expectations. It's the mistakes we've made before as prodigals that fueled the fire to never run aimless again. It's the scars on our hearts from the course of a purposeless dating lifestyle that propelled our eyes forward to the actual aim of dating, which is marriage.

If singleness is the cue to get your life ready and marriage is the finish line (for this season at least), then dating is like the starting block. It's the starting blocks propelling us forward into a relationship with one aim in mind, marriage, the finish line. But how many of us get stuck in a treadmill like loop? Never making it to commitment. Never making it to a real relationship. Never making it to engaged. Somehow making it to sitting down at a coffee shop talking about why it's been three years, two apartments, one kid later and what the heck does our future together have in store? No aim. No goal. No intentionality.

I know I was there before. And it felt hopeless. That's why it was a breath of fresh air, after years of sprinting nowhere, when Peyton flat out said, "I don't date just to date." Because after all the crap I've seen, I made the decision to take my marks, set my aim and never date just for the hell of it again. Aimlessly running from one unhealthy place to the next.

Have you made this decision yet in your heart or maybe your relationship together? Have you set your aim higher? Let's face it; dating in a biblical way is exhausting (we'll talk more on combating fatigue later). But God knows how much more difficult running the race of your life can be when you set your mark on Jesus. Especially because there's opposition against that path. But no matter what your relational status is, run the good race, don't run aimlessly anymore. Run so you may win the prize. Forget what lies behind and strain forward to what lies ahead. Press on to the goal for the prize of the upward call of God in Christ. Shake off every weight and sin that holds you down and run with endurance the race set before you. Keeping your aim on Jesus. He endured the cross and overcame sin and death. He can and will help you endure this race of life, of intentionally living. You're surrounded by such a huge crowd of witnesses cheering you and me on. Don't disqualify yourself. Trust and wait on the Lord, he'll renew your strength. You'll run, but not grow weary. At times all you might be able to do is put one foot in front of the other; but keep walking! You won't faint! With God that collapsing free fall of exhaustion will turn into soaring and mounting up on wings like eagles! Keep moving forward towards Christ. He'll help you crawl, he'll help you walk, run, sprint; and he'll even help you soar exceedingly abundant above all you expected in this life.

Individual Devotional (15 Minutes)

1) Can you think of any friends who keep running *aimlessly*, never making it any further in life? Can this be said about your dating experience?

   a) Why or why not?

2) Could your current relationship or former relationship categorize as *aimless*?

3) Who in your life would say it does have aim, who in your life would say it doesn't?

   a) And why would they say that?

Couples Devotional (15 Minutes)

1) How can we start to bring better aim and intentional goals into our relationship for our relationship?

   a) What would those goals/aims be?

2) How can you stand firm in these goals and decisions? What are the plans and steps for seeing them through?

3) Who can help you identify some of these next steps you may need to start taking or prepare to take?

   a) When can you sit down with them next?

Application
Record these goals in your Prayer Journal along with how and when
you'd like to accomplish them.

Chapter 12

Skeletons

[25] So stop telling lies. Let us tell our neighbors the truth, for we
are all parts of the same body. - Ephesians 4:25
Also read Ephesians 4:15 / John 8:44 / James 5:16 / Isaiah 53:5 /
Philippians 3:13

One of the hardest parts of being intentional when you date isn't
the notion of being clear and upfront in your current relationship, but
also being clear and upfront about the things in your past. Let me ask you
an unfair question; if you dumped your entire dating or relational or
prodigal or just flat out sinful skeletons out of the closet of your past into
your current relationship, would your significant other choose to stay?
Like I said, an unfair question.

I know we like to put our best foot forward when it comes to
going on that first date. We filter our words, analyze our every thought
and sift out just the right amount of things to say about ourselves. And as
time passes, slowly but surely we reveal more and more of who we are as
we begin to filter less and less. Until finally, the real, unfiltered, unaltered
you is presented. Yet no matter how close you get, or how much time has
passed, most people have a point and place in their past they choose *not*
to reveal. We keep pushing the secrets back and the skeletons deep
down and locked away for good. Out of the light of day and transparency.

But the problem with telling half-truths or not the full truth is that
it's unbiblical. Not only when it comes to others, but especially when it
comes to your potential significant other. Ephesians 4:25 tells us
"Therefore laying aside falsehood, speak truth each one of you with his
neighbor, for we are members of one another." And Jesus takes it to a
whole another level when he tells a particular group of Jews "You are
children of your father (the devil), and you love to do the evil things he
does... He has always hated the truth, because there is no truth in him.
When he lies it is consistent with his character: for he is a liar and the
father of lies." Ouch! You see, the problem with half-truths is that they're
actually not the real truth. And the problem with white lies is that they're
still lies. Which leaves us at a crossroads when it comes to dating in a

Jesus centered way and being intentional. We can be like our Father in heaven and present the *truth in love*, or we can be like the father of lies and try to keep those skeletons buried.

This was probably one of the hardest conversations I ever had to have. As Peyton and I kept getting closer and closer to each other, talking more and more, I knew this conversation was coming. I knew that being intentional was taking us to this crossroads. Being honest and forthcoming about our past, or choosing to keep those secrets buried. I don't judge anyone who's ever chosen half-truths or white lies about their past; looking someone you care immensely about deep in their eyes while revealing the mire and filth of your life before them is brutal. That crushed look on their face as a lifetime of skeletons comes barreling down out of the closet of regret. It's one of the most painful things you'll do. Letting them know just how broken you are or were. Does being intentional or successful relationally really require that?

Before I talk more on how that conversation went for us, let me tell you about this intentional conversation in another couples life that never got started. It was a few years in, and one kid later. Shauna and Larry are finally engaged and looking to pull the trigger. They did the usual American routine, had a couple kids each from prior flings and marriages, started dating each other, eventually moved in together, had a kid together and is now looking to tie the knot. They were about to start their future together, but the problem was they never actually talked about the past. Neither of them were *perfect*, obviously, yet they continued to play house together without ever laying anything *too deep* out on the table. They just tried to keep the past buried and the skeletons in the closet. Yet scripture's promise came to pass from Numbers 23:32, Beware your sins, they're sure to find you. And find them they did.

And like all half-truths and white lies weaved together, with the tug of one little lie like string, the whole ensemble unravels. And something from Shauna's past surfaced from a third party. And when it did, one ugly truth after another came falling down on top of Larry, the tapestry of lies undone. Skeleton after skeleton came toppling down. And the strangest part is that some of the *unforgivable* things in Shauna's life he resented her for, were some of the same things in his life he'd done as well. He couldn't forgive her, even though they both played house and went to church. He actually despised the skeletons she had, even though he had the exact same ones in his closet too.

Which takes me back to that unfair question I asked, would your significant other choose to stay? The foundation of Shauna's and Larry's relationship was feeble. Good intentions, high hopes and the corpses of sinful living from their past mortared together and glazed over with a shiny coat of half-truths. Four years, one family, and several childhoods completely shaken. It reminds me of what Jesus said when he tells us to build our lives on a solid foundation. And this applies to our dating and relational lives as well. I know what I had to do if I ever wanted our relationship to last. And so did Peyton.

After dating for several weeks, we meet up at Starbucks. The coffee was great but my stomach was in knots. She said she had something to say first. And it felt like a mac-truck was parked on my gut, the pressure collapsing my lungs, unable to fully breathe. We opened up the closet of ugly truth and skeleton bones. She went first. I could barely listen. I wanted so bad to retreat to the blissful ignorance in my head. She could barely stay strong and not cry. Unsure if I would ever love her or even move forward with her. And then it was my turn to go. How do you tell someone you're falling in love with about all the gory corpses of failure and sin you've left a cemetery full of in your past and look them right in the eye about it? Now it felt like that mac truck on my stomach was set on fire by the disappointment in our tone.

There we were, being honest. One hundred percent completely honest and transparent. Pulling skeleton after skeleton out of our closets until we filled an entire valley with dry bones. It sucked.

But the strange thing is our God loves to do incredible things with dry bones. Check that, God loves to do *miraculous* things with the skeletons of our past we let the world see. Just as the Lord commanded Ezekiel to speak life, so too we as Christ followers, surrounded in a world of dead and broken people are not to condemn, but speak words of life! Raising hope from the graves of the past. Exhuming joy from the tombs of regret. And as God commanded Ezekiel to speak a prophetic message to the wind, so too we are to incite the winds of grace, and mercy, and forgiveness, and reconciliation into the walking dead we encounter daily. Yes, when you are entrenched by sin and death and the foul smell of a thousand broken mistakes, don't condemn someone to the second death, speak life! Speak hope! Speak joy to every soul! Death where is your sting? Skeletons, hollow and void of life abundant, listen to the word of the Lord, "Look! I am going to put breath into you and make you live again! I will put flesh and muscles on you and cover you with skin. I will put breath into you and you will come to life! Then you will know that I am the Lord!"

And that is exactly what Peyton did. Entrenched in our sin from the past, Peyton spoke life. She spoke a message of hope. She brought it back around to Jesus. That no, she's not proud of her mistakes; but she is no longer a slave to them! She is no longer a slave to guilt and shame! Those hurts her heart has accumulated have been healed. It's because of Jesus that the broken fragments of our lives are brought back together for good and not for evil. As Isaiah prophesied in Isaiah 53:5, "He was pierced for our transgressions, he was crushed for our iniquities; the punishment that brought us peace was on him, and by his wounds we are healed." By his wounds we are healed. You can be healed.

She spoke mercy, she spoke grace. She trusted the work of the Holy Spirit to bring life into our future just like he brought life to Jesus from the grave. And we left that conversation enlivened, forgetting the past and looking forward to what lies ahead.

Now back to that unfair question. It's your choice. You can build on a solid foundation and be intentional, be transparent and be honest. Or you can try to keep that valley of skeleton bones hidden. Try to keep them buried. But beware your sins, they are sure to find you.

Individual Devotional (15 Minutes)

1) If you are in a relationship, what are some skeletons you need to get

   completely out in the open this week? (If not what are some

   skeletons you will have to get out in your next relationship?)

   a) What are you afraid others might say if they knew?

2) Are you or would you be ready for a conversation like this? What

   would you be afraid they might possibly reveal? What seems

   unforgivable to you?

3) Would you be ready to forgive and pardon and give grace? If not what

   does that say about your relationship with Christ?

Couples Devotional (15 Minutes)

1) Prepare your hearts and pray together first. Leave a piece of paper on

   the table, don't write anything on it, but let it symbolize a recording

   of all your sins. And when you're done with this conversation, ask for

   forgiveness, pray Christ will bring you breakthrough and healing and

   then throw away or destroy this piece of paper.

   a) Start this honest and intentional conversation about your

      skeletons.

Application
Take that paper, make a fire in your in your fireplace or fire pit outside, or just find a shredder. Ask God to heal your hearts from the past, thank him for his forgiveness, grace and reconciliation. And ask him to let this moment be a moment where you two start brand new in Christ as a couple. And destroy that recording of your wrongs forgiven in Christ!

Chapter 13

Prayer

[16] Always be joyful. [17] Never stop praying. [18] Be thankful in all circumstances, for this is God's will for you who belong to Christ Jesus.
- 1 Thessalonians 5:16-18
Also read James 4:8 / Psalms 118 / Isaiah 46:9-10 / James 5:16 / Hebrews 4:16

A person's prayer life reveals a lot about the condition of their heart. How they interact with God, what they think about him, how often they'd like to interact with him and actually do, and so on. But it's my belief that a couple's prayer life, or lack thereof, reveals even more about the condition of their relationship more than anything else. Praying together as a couple is just as vital to a healthy and lasting relationship as your heart beat is vital to living. As a pastor, being immersed with people from all different demographics and their various life stories, I can tell you this about divorce and separation; somewhere among all the case by case variables leading up to it lays a common thread. That thread being one or both people stopped earnestly praying for and or with each other. And if you as a couple want to be intentional, not just with each other, but intentionally grounded in Christ; praying for one another is just as vital as breathing.

I'll never forget the first time Peyton and I prayed together. We were about to head out on our second date and we stopped to pick up some frozen yogurt. We were there in the parking lot, sitting in the car. Right before we left, I looked over at her, reached out my hand and asked, "Would you like to pray with me?"

Lightning struck our car as we became hand in hand... at least that's what it felt like. For the first time ever Peyton and I were hand in hand praying to our Father. Unified with one heart inviting him to be with us, to lead us, and guide us on this journey. And there's something powerful about two children of God, actually coming together and dedicating themselves to him. There's something powerful about participating in God's will coming to pass on this earth. It's incredible, awe-invoking, like the first time you've seen a tornado in person, or a volcano erupt. There is something indescribably powerful about letting the kingdom of heaven advance through you.

And I wish I could say every prayer has always felt that electrifying every single time. But they haven't. As the time passed we would have seasons come and go with an abundance in prayer or more scarcity in prayer. And it's in those rocky, awful and painful times I learned all the valuable lessons why prayer is essential. And why it needs to start in dating. Here are some of those differences being intentional with prayer can make.

Presence. James 4:8 tells us to "Come close to God and he will come close to you." And Jesus (the apostle James' half-brother) tells us in Matthew 18:20 "Where two or more are gathered in my name, I am there with them." Start praying together as a couple today, or from even before the relationship officially begins. <u>Because when you invite Jesus to be with you as two people intentionally seeking after him, he is</u>. When you pray together you invite him to work more freely in your relationship. Remember, "Where the spirit of the lord is there is freedom" (2 Corinthians 13:7). So invite God to be the Lord of your relationship through continuous prayer together and watch him *free* you from all the dating snares you've gotten entangled in before. Watch him *free* you up from all of the dating pitfalls you fallen in before.

Patient Endurance. Psalms 118:1 reminds us to "Give thanks to the Lord, for he is good! His faithful love *endures forever*." We can bank on that promise by looking at Jesus' *proof-of-love* on the cross. The proof which solidifies the New Covenant hope we have. And 1 Thessalonians 5:17-18 tells us to "Never stop praying. Be thankful in *all your circumstances* for this is God's will for you who belong in Christ." We can see from the law based Old Covenant, to the grace based New Covenant signed with Jesus' blood, God remains good and faithful, no matter what our circumstances are. There are going to be situations and circumstances and people and spiritual attack that will oppose your newly forming relationship. Especially when it's Christ centered. That is why you will need to pray together continuously! Don't let bleak circumstances define your outlook. Let the cross define your perspective. Dating and finding the one isn't a perfect process, but God is perfect. <u>Look at your circumstances through the lens of his love and watch what he can do when you patiently endure</u>!

Healing. James 5:16 tells us to "Confess our sins to each other, and pray for each other that you might be healed. The earnest prayer of a righteous person has great power and produces wonderful results." When it comes to getting close to people and getting in a relationship, you're going to get hurt. A LOT. It's a fact of this broken world. And now being married and having our fair share of fights, this verse looks a lot less like a suggestion, and more like conflict resolution. You're going to hurt one another somehow, someway. You need to reconcile every time by being honest, speaking the truth in love, confessing your sins, how you were in the wrong (even when you were in the right) and you need to pray for healing together.

Control. Isaiah 46:9-10 entreats us to "Remember the things I (God) have done in the past. For I alone am God! I am God and there is none like me. Only I can tell you the future before it even happens. Everything I plan will come to pass, for I do whatever I wish." During hard times this verse isn't easy to fathom, but there's no doubt if you can reconcile the fact that there is a God, it's obvious he is in control. And that's good for your relationship. At times all hell will break loose and you won't know which way is right or wrong, up or down. You won't know if you should stay together or hop the next train outta town. You won't be able to decide if they make you the happiest or the most frustrated person on earth (most likely both). But pause, reflect on God. He is in control. Trust in him, pray together. You're not in this alone. He has your back! And if God is for your relationship what can be against you!?

Help. Hebrews 4:16 tells us "So let us come boldly to the throne of our gracious God. There we will receive his mercy and we will find grace *to help us when we need it most*." From conflict to temptations, you're going to need help to make it together in this world. Supernatural help! One of the best ways to come before the throne is together in prayer. You will need the help and the strength of God almighty if you are going to become the man or woman God's called you to be. Including the man or woman your future spouse and family will need you to be. Don't push through the hell of this world without the king of heaven by your side. Pray for help constantly, every single day, together.

There is so much more I wish I could dive into, but that would have to be a face to face conversation. After learning these lessons the hard way, I can honestly say me and Peyton pray together every single day. Late to work or on the run, we make praying together a priority. We can't afford not to. You can't afford not to. Spend two weeks praying together every single day, and watch the difference it makes. You'll see the difference being intentional in prayer creates. <u>You might unintentionally be keeping the relationship together with prayer, where all your other ones have fallen apart</u>. Have you ever thought about that before?

Individual Devotional (15 Minutes)

1) How would you describe your prayer life?

2) Do you believe it's important for you and your future wife or husband to pray together?

   a) Why or why not?

3) What might it look like to let the kingdom advance through you in your current situations and place in life? How can you align your prayers with Gods will? Look it up if you need ideas.

4) Have you ever prayed earnestly and often in other relationships? What might that say about its importance to your current or future relationship?

5) How might you personally need God's help through the power of his Holy Spirit in your life to step up and become the man or woman he has called you to be and your future family needs you to be?

Couples Devotional (15 Minutes)

1) How would we describe our prayer life together?

2) Might there be a correlation between how our prayer life together is going and how our relationship is going?

3) In what ways are we participating in God's will coming to pass here

on earth?

   a) Have you ever thought about it that way?

4) What's stopping us from praying together daily?

5) What are some of the ways we've hurt each other before, or keep

hurting one another, how can we reconcile these hurts through

prayer?

Application
Chose a designated time that works best for you two, maybe in the morning, afternoon, or evening. And for the next week, maybe in person or over the phone, pray for one another.

Chapter 14

Affection

[12] You say, "I am allowed to do anything"—but not everything is good for you. And even though "I am allowed to do anything," I must not become a slave to anything. [13] You say, "Food was made for the stomach, and the stomach for food." (This is true, though someday God will do away with both of them.) But you can't say that our bodies were made for sexual immorality. They were made for the Lord, and the Lord cares about our bodies. - 1 Corinthians 6:12-13
Also read 1 Corinthians 7:2 / 1 Corinthians 6:18 / 2 Corinthians 6:3 /
1 Corinthians 8:9 / 1 Corinthians 15:5 / Galatians 5:13

Affection is one of the few aspects of dating that people are actually intentional about. Unfortunately it's usually being intentional about doing the *wrong* things. Now, we too as Christ followers are meant to be intentional when it comes to affection and dating, except in the right ways of course. Unless we end up somewhere we didn't intend to go.

We as Christ followers have been told full well to *run from sexual sin, because no other sin so clearly affects us as this one does*. Maybe that's why it's the most fun to us as broken beings; because it's the most destructive. Which is why we need to be intentional about it when dating.

When it comes to affection, we can't run from this conversation. No matter how awkward it might seem, as a couple you will have to sit down over some coffee or food and draw the line. Notice we're told to *run from* sexual immorality. And just like a race, you will have to set the course if you're going to get to the finish line, married and in the spiritual confines of sexual fulfillment.

You have to sit down, converse, and start talking your way from sex backwards; talking about what's unacceptable to happen. Because sexual immorality doesn't start at the finish line of intercourse. Sexual immorality begins at the starting point of uncontainable desire. The starting point of sexual immorality is the point in physical affection when you can't hold back your desires any further and now it's a race to get each other's clothes off. Sexual immorality doesn't start with sex; it starts with those *points of no return* that fire the gun of uncontrolled desire.

And this where the legalists go nuts because it's different for every couple. It could be a kiss that does it. It could be making out that starts it. Perhaps spooning is the button that gets those gears going. I knew a couple that felt so convicted, anything past holding hands was considered too far. <u>Whatever *act* shatters the dam of resolve, holding back the waters of lust and desire, that's the line that you can't cross</u>. Because once you cross it, you usually sprint to the finish line of sex before you even realize it.

I remember sitting across from Peyton at Starbucks (which by now you can tell is my second home), and we just laid it all out there. Sex ain't gonna happen. But we also knew the wide variety of *on-ramps* that takes us there (as do you). And so we laid out the boundaries, we drew a hard line. We still showed affection in pleasant/healthy ways. But we knew where not to go and we knew what could take us there too. Don't tolerate those little harmless steps further in affection. Run from them. Because even the most firm perimeters agreed upon are easily traversed the moment your dam of resolve crumbles.

You can't survive without these upfront conversations. The fight to flee from the heat of the moment, and not draw closer like a moth to the flame is hard enough as it is. Without clear indicators, and established perimeters to keep you intentionally away from sex, you'll end up underneath sheets that tell of regret without ever realizing what they'll witness.

By now I'm sure this is starting to sound like grandma's old-school lecture. But from one couple who's gone through this to another in the midst of it; let me tell you plainly, it feels less like a nice little run or stroll away from temptation and more like a bare-knuckle, back alley street fight for survival. A knock out, beat down of temptation and desire. It's a bloody-as-hell battle. And being in this day and age, you have more guns pointed at you, than with you. It feels like war, and war is hell. And all hell is against you. But don't worry, remember what Jesus said, *The gates of hell shall not conquer his church*. And notice the Bible describes that *we are the church* (1 Corinthians 12:27). And the gates of hell can't conquer our resolve if we are intentionally surrendering our lives, our affections, and our purpose together as a couple to Christ!

We'll talk more about the purpose behind not having sex other than these practical tips in our section about purpose. <u>Because life lived in purpose trumps life lived in fear of impurity</u>.

Individual Devotional (15 Minutes)

1) Have you ever sat down in your current relationship or past

   relationships and drew a hardline when it comes to permissible

   affections?

   a) Why did you or why didn't you?

2) What's your *starting point*? And how can you stop from getting

   there?

3) When was the last time you experienced an immense amount of

   temptation and desire all at once?

Couples Devotional (15 Minutes)

1) Have we had this conversation before on appropriate affection?

2) What are the triggers and things that push you past the *point of no*

   return?

3) What are some boundaries we have put in place, or should put in

   place?

4) What is your main reason for avoiding and fleeing from

   temptation/sex?

   a) Is it rooted in Christian priorities? Or is it rooted in your eternal

      purpose as a Child of God? What's the difference?

5) How can you start to put these boundaries in place today, and refocus

your attention on why we flee from temptation?

Application

Hopefully by now, there is a Christ centered couple you are close with. Share with them these boundaries and ask them to help you stay accountable and ask them constantly pray for you two.

A Transition

Chapter 15

Monuments

Read Joshua Chapter 3 – Chapter 4:7

As we prepare to dive into our third section, *Purpose*, I wanted to make some space for this transition from *Intentional*. If you picked up this book as a devotional for you and your girlfriend or boyfriend to help bring direction to your dating journey, this chapter is just for you.

As we dive in further, I want to lay out some makers on this dating journey we all can recognize. The first marker when it comes to dating is *talking*. Before you ever start going on dates, you simply talk with that person, right? Is there chemistry, are they weird, do you like-like them, or just plainly like them? Pertinent questions like these you've pondered over for hours.

The next universal marker I believe applies to everyone and can be agreed on by everyone is *dating*. You went from a place of just talking to now going on dates with that person. The movies, the fair, out to dinner, ice skating, you name it. I believe this part of the dating journey is easily identified. But what comes after dating is the tricky part for some to navigate. This next part has made things confusion for this entire generation.

In a relationship, Thank you Facebook for making this simpler for our generation to grasp. If I put forth the question to you, is it serious? An indicator for you to fall back on is *Facebook official*. If it is serious, then you would reply yes, we're Facebook official. But if it's not too serious this indicator will be absent.

Now guys let me ask you this question, is that *it*? If you like or love this girl enough, then you guess you might as well pull the trigger and change your status? For the woman who very well might be your match made in heaven, who God has been preparing for you your whole life and vice-verse, and all you have in response to that once in a lifetime phenomenon is clicking a button on the internet?! No wonder this *marker* is where our relationships hit a snare and/or are fatally wounded.

we've turned our commitment, our devotion, and our response to how incredible it is to finally be with someone you can see yourself potentially marrying into a click of a button...

Things have obviously changed since Bible times. Especially since the times of ancient Israel. Devotion and dedication and other things of this magnitude weren't taken lightly by them or by God and his relationship to them. We see from the very beginning of God reestablishing his relationship with us broken humans through Abraham that things got real. Things got real, real quick. To symbolize Abraham's commitment and devotion to the covenant God was establishing, he had to cut off his foreskin! And all of his children's foreskins too! And their children's foreskins; even till today! That's a lot of foreskin! And throughout the ages they've continued in this covenant.

Not only did they cling to circumcision as their sign of a relationship with God through their ancestors, which was one of the things they *could* control as slaves in Egypt. But as the time passed, they've covered the Middle East with monuments and milestones in their relational journey with Yahweh. Perhaps one of the most significant monuments to be found was the one built from the rocks at the bottom of the miraculously dried Jordan River.

Joshua chapter three is a big moment for the people of Israel! Some scholars believe their numbers got up into the millions as they left Egypt and wandered for forty years! And it's there the nation was camped beside the Jordan River, the only thing separating them from the land promised to them for centuries. But this wasn't a stream when they got there, it was overflowing! I've heard some pastor's reference a few scholars who believed the Jordan could have even been about a mile wide at times of overflow like this. So God does what only he could do and he instructs Joshua to have the priests pick up the Ark of the Covenant and go step into the river and watch as God stops the waters and dries it up down to the river bed. Sure enough, they obey and God controls the outcome just like he said.

Picture that, some priest holding a gold box standing in the middle of the what should be overflowing Jordan River as potentially millions of God's people go by. And it gets even crazier! To further show off as only God can, he also instructs Joshua to have twelve men gather twelve large stones from the river bed where the priest are standing during this unfathomable event and bring them out to build a monument to remember this day! And sure enough they do! The scripture mentions it was still standing by the time this event was recorded and written down into text.

God was intentional in his relationship with the Israelites and he never took an opportunity to do something incredible for granted. Because he knew what it would mean and symbolize to his people when the hard times in front of them ensued.

I wonder how many relationships have to lose their way, have to fall by the wayside and end up sunk before we start to figure out that doing remarkable things weren't just beneficial as a thing of the past? <u>How many of us guys will miss out on the opportunities to do something unusually big and go all out on our dating journeys</u>? How many of us are going to let incredible opportunities float by instead of picking up some stones and commemorating taking the next step in your relationship and make it official? Girls, are you going to continue to settle and go around the relational bend again and again with another guy who says, "Sure, we can make it Facebook official, I guess?" Don't you want a guy who thinks you're worth it enough to go back out there and grab those rocks!? Don't you want a man with some stones to go back into the riverbed where the flood waters can come crashing down at any moment, and do something special?

I wonder how terrified the enemy spies must have been seeing this event unfold. I wonder how hopeless they felt when they had to report that the Israelite God even gave them time enough to send twelve guys into the riverbed again and pick up twelve individual large stones one at a time to build a monument. I wonder how terrified the future opposition must have been when they saw the monument and what it represented standing tall; the story it told of God's immense, supernatural commitment to his people, and their life-risking commitment to him?

<u>I wonder how terrified the enemy of our souls and Godly relationships must feel when we get intentional and take the time and effort to commemorate what God is doing in our lives and in our relationship together</u>. I wonder how much strength and resolve monuments like this gave God's people when they endured future trials and tribulations in their pursuit of claiming their promised land. I wonder how inspired, how steely their resolve must have been looking back on those monuments and remembering the awe and wonder of water

drying up, the potent smell of river moss in their nose as they crossed and even the feeling of riverbed mud in their sandals and toes?

It makes me wonder how much stronger our relationships would be as we endure the future trials in the pursuit of reaching the promised places together in our relationship journey if we had monuments like this to look back on? Imagine if you could look back during the trials and remember the chill of being a thousand feet up in a hot air balloon, or the sound of the waves crashing on a sunset picnic for two, or even the simplicity of being able to look back and feel the warmth of the sun that day you were doing something fun and made it official. What fruit might we be missing out on by not asking that simple question; do you want to take the next step with me? Or even, will you be my girlfriend? It might sound stupid nowadays, *I know*. I'm pretty sure twelve guys and twelve stones each might have sounded pretty stupid back then too with the waters potentially crashing at any time.

But there's something powerful about being intentional. <u>There's something powerful when we make externally visible declarations with our lives in front of God and others of what we're experiencing internally</u>. Maybe think back to your baptism as a Christ follower before you think about how about stupid this is seems. That outward declaration of an inward faith and devotion you experience.

And I'd have to admit, part of me always had a thought of doubt or hesitation when it came to doing big things for Peyton and our relationship together. Part of me wondered if buying dozens of candles, making a special mix with our song, and eliciting the help of a friend to get us on top of the tallest building in our little town was a bit overboard just to ask her to be my girlfriend. Part of me felt pretty silly renting a limo, asking her to take off work so she could take the afternoon and get all fancy wearing her prom dress. I felt especially silly when I asked a volunteer and friend to meet us at the trendy prom-picture location in town and take photos of us before we headed off to dinner for two in our prom outfits and limo; then dance the night away at a place I decorated the entire day of. Just so I can right the wrong of her never being swept off of her feet and asked to prom by a guy she's head over heels for. Heck, I even wondered if picking her up at 4:30am and driving to a nearby vineyard was a little crazy, just so we can go up on a sunrise hot air balloon tour of Temecula's wine country and pop the question. I asked her to be my girlfriend above hundreds of rooftops in our valley, so I figured I needed to be above thousands to ask her to be my wife.

Part of me always had the slight inkling, is this too much, or is this stupid? In today's world sure, maybe it was a *little much*. But at the end of the day, when we can look back on those photos, the answer is no. And that is our testimony when it comes to being intentional and doing something special for our commitment to each other. And even if you think your relationship is somehow different, and you don't need a grand gesture like that, look at Israel. Just about every world power in the history of man has come against them, conquered them, crushed them and or tried to genocide them as a nation and people out of existence. The Egyptians, The Amalekites, the Philistines, the Assyrians, the Babylonians, the Persians, the Greeks, the Romans, the surrounding Islamic nations, even the Nazis! Yet sure enough, here they are, still going strong. I wonder if your future together will endure like that? It's your choice.

Grand gestures might be too much. And asking her to *be your gal, and go steady* might be too old fashioned. But there is something powerful about external declarations representing internal commitments. There's something powerful about having big moments together. Moments you can look back on when things get hard. Monuments, I guess you can call them.

Individual Devotional (15 Minutes)

1) What has your track record looked like in the past when it comes to more than just dating and making it official?

2) Have you ever been stuck in that awkward place between dating and in a relationship? How did you bring clarity to that last situation? Do you need to do that now?

3) How many opportunities have you let float by to do something special to commemorate your relationship, or the start of it?

Couples Devotional (15 Minutes)

1) When it comes to going on dates, or being in a relationship, where is our relationship currently?

   a) Where do you want it to be?

2) What would we say is the state of our relationship officially? And what is our commitment level to each other?

3) How important do you think making it official is when it comes to navigating all of the future challenges of being together?

Application
Make a list of at least twelve things you'd love to do together this year and do them once a month.

Section 3 Overview

Purpose

[9] (God) Who hath saved us and called us according to his own purpose and grace which was given to us in Christ Jesus before time began.
- 2 Timothy 1:9
Also read Ecclesiastes 3:11

There are many things wrong about the world we live in today. You don't have to believe in God to know it's true. But amongst all the things Christians say about this world; sinners, gentiles, abominations, heathens, Satan's flying monkeys, you name it. I think the judgment is harsher than the crime. I tend to think the world is just dehydrated in a sense.

It's dehydrated of purpose. Its void of purpose and quenching for the living waters only Christ can provide in this life. One of the paramount verses in my life is 2 timothy 1:9, "(God) Who hath saved us and called us according to his own purpose and grace which was given to us in Christ Jesus before time began." With this verse in mind it makes sense as to why it's hell breaking loose on the news daily. The world is living void and absent from heavenly purpose. No wonder this country's priorities are skewed, they're void of purpose, an eternal purpose. A void of purpose that sin always fills.

We may not all be ax murderers or arsonists or the *worst sinners* ever, but why do our lives as Christ followers encompass more of the hell we see in the world around us then the constitutes of heaven we read in scripture? I truly believe a major part of it comes down to purpose, or the lack thereof in our lives.

Purpose is something you don't grasp at first try. And purpose is even harder to bestow or convey, especially to developing adults. As a middle school pastor it is really easy for me and my team to give these kids Christian priorities instead. Scary easy as a matter of fact. It's too simple to stand on a stage or sit in a small group and list off a set of priorities these kids need to have if they will consider themselves Christian. And the most frightful part of all is that all those Christian priorities we can rapid fire like an assault rifle are actually good for them.

In a sense, we can demolish kids in the droves with Christian priorities like Rambo's *Final Blood,* and actually receive psychological gratification for our efforts since those priorities are *good* for them. Even though an empty religion of priorities is even more dangerous to their souls then violence in video games.

Fortunately and unfortunately, human beings are hardwired for something greater than just good or moral priorities. We're created and redeemed for a purpose. A purpose from before time began, an eternal purpose. Maybe that's why the scripture mentions God has placed eternity in our hearts? And growing up I was never connected enough in youth group to catch that this is what they were conveying. I was never rooted enough to see the glimmer of something deeper in the scriptures.

I caught the surface level commandments, *all ten* believe it or not. Which were impossible priorities back then for God's people, so I'm not too sure why we're still holding unbelievers to those standards today. I even caught the more in-depth priorities like why hormonally explosive teenage boys aren't to masturbate because some guy, so many thousands of years ago, *spilled his seed* on the floor, instead of impregnating his wife. A story so violently abused out of context it's like a handgun of moral priority fired blatantly. Plainly put, it's easy to convey Christian priorities, but we were made for something more.

Perhaps Christian priorities are what you were given as a kid, maybe you didn't go to church at all. No matter how you grew up or what your background is, every human being is faced with the same question. What is my purpose?

Maybe you just graduated college and you're finally *on your own,* except for those few bills mom still helps you pay. Or possibly your thirty-two and living in your parents basement. The questions remain the same, what will you do in this life? What is your purpose? What is your calling? Is it really as empty as the major you're educated in? Is it really as crushing as that entry level position your career is hindered on? What's your purpose? Why are you here on this planet? Why were you born?

Sadly enough, the world never really slows down enough to care. It's satisfied with vain pursuits of all kinds. It's focused on a plethora of empty priorities. But if we as Christ followers never slow down enough, or put away the distractions in order to discover our purposes, how are our lives any different than the world around us? We might spend the rest of our lives just short of the abundance Christ has in store for us according to his purpose.

Imagine if you can that each and every human has been instilled with a calling and purpose from before time began. Imagine every person being capable of discovering a calling in their life with eternal implications. Imagine every man, woman and child able to impact eternity in their own unique way according to Christ's purposes. Now how hollow are the Christian priorities and the pursuits this world prescribes? The ones we settle for.

Being a pastor of middle school ministry, I'm usually too late. These kids have been spoon-fed the priorities of this culture for more than ten years now. Their consumed by it, defined by it, sold out to it. Sometimes setting themselves so far from the eternal value placed in them they turn to the drugs they steal from their parents medicine cabinet. They experiment with different experiences to try to satisfy their uncontainable emotions and desires, longing to feel something more. Or they even try to escape through self-harm and suicide, something they've seen hundreds of times on television. How can they find their purpose? How can we?

I believe the answer is in the question, <u>we have to find it</u>. We discover it. Under layer after layer, we have to peel off the priorities and pursuits and promises this world has instilled in us. And every step closer to our creator is another step closer to the calling and purpose we were created for. Before the world ever told you how to act or how to live; before this world even began spinning, there was and is and will forever be beyond time and space a creator who designed you with a purpose. And it's our adventure in this life to discover what that is. An adventure meant to be lived out together.

Individual Devotional (15 Minutes)

1) When it comes to purpose, can you say you've been living with

   purpose or living with a purpose?

2) Looking back on your relationship with God over the years, was it

   mostly based on rules to follow? Or has it felt like something more?

3) How often do you slow down to think and reflect about what God is

   doing or wanting to do in your life?

4) What are some pursuits or priorities of this world you're chasing after

   that might run counter or hinder what Christ is wanting to do in your

   life?

Couples Devotional (15 Minutes)

1) Have you given much thought to your purpose in this life? Why or

   why not?

2) What was your upbringing like in regards to Christianity?

   a) How might that impact or influence your current faith?

3) What might be some of the *Christian priorities* you're focusing

   intensely on so you can excuse the other areas of your life still not

   surrendered to Christ? Like morning devotions, or prayer groups, or not drinking, yet still blatantly living in/or allowing sin in some other

areas of life.

4) What did you answer for question four in the Individual Devotional

Application
Spend one hour a day this week, or a five hour chunk of time and reflect on those deeper questions in this life. Reflect on your life and ask God questions, pray about his purposes in your life and utilize scripture.

Chapter 16

The Great Co-mission

[18] Jesus came and told his disciples, "I have been given all authority in heaven and on earth.
[19] Therefore, go and make disciples of all the nations, baptizing them in the name of the Father and the Son and the Holy Spirit. [20] Teach these new disciples to obey all the commands I have given you. And be sure of this: I am with you always, even to the end of the age."
- Matthew 28:18-20
Also read Mark 16:14-20 / Luke 24:35-53 / Acts 1:4-9

I wonder if James Bond woke up one day and thought to himself, "I should be a secret agent/assassin." It was probably at freshman orientation at his local Community College; that drove me pretty nuts too. How did he stumble upon this calling? No doubt he is seemingly called for it! The spy of all spies, out foxing anyone and everyone! Granted, James bond is probably not the best analogy when talking about our calling as Christians. A murderer with a license to kill, a sexual deviant for the thrill, and the will to do just about anything else you can think of just for the heck of it. But still, it's been how many decades, how many movies, how many Bond's, James Bonds and we're still enthralled?

There's something enthralling about an all or nothing mission. There's something enamoring about an all-out, jump out of a plane, run on top of a train, and flip your car going ninety miles per hour type of mission. The types of missions that take you so far out of your comfort zone you're dangling out of helicopters, sitting at a high stakes poker game, or even parkouring in a sinking structure in Venice. And most of us might not ever partake on a life or death secret mission to save the world as we know it. But the truth is we're called for a mission with even greater importance! An eternal mission, a co-mission.

When Jesus first found the twelve disciples, it's needless to say they were without a calling. Sure, some of them believed their calling was to be fishermen. While others were so lost when it came what to do with their lives they ended up working for the enemy of the state, the Romans. If Jesus would have never selected them, their lives may have never altered. Their current life's calling would have simply sufficed. But they did encounter Jesus and their lives were never the same!

I wonder if John knew right away he would be called the disciple of love and his words that he was inspired to write in John chapter three verse sixteen would contain one of the most pertinent lines in all of eternity? I wonder if Simon knew that day, the first time he met Jesus, he would soon be called *rock* and his life would be foundational for the birth of the church and its explosion in this world? Or if Saul knew the moment he was knocked down and blinded by a light from heaven that Jesus would call him to be the catalyst for taking his message of hope and salvation to the gentile nations? Probably not.

I'm willing to bet the moment you gave your life to Jesus or encountered him or got baptized you didn't exactly know every single detail about what your life's calling would entail either. Or what your life's purpose might be? Neither did I, or my wife, or really anyone else I've ever met. <u>This is probably why Jesus gives us a mission to carry out before we ever find our calling to live out.</u> And not just any mission. A great mission! The most important mission any man or mankind has ever received. A mission with eternal implications. A co-mission!

The great co-mission, as Pastor Brian Houston coins it. A mission meant to be embarked on together with others! A mission that instills a pursuit for our calling. A mission that reveals your God-ordained purpose. And as a couple, it's a mission meant to be lived out together!

Your relationship isn't meant just for you two and your happiness. Just as our lives belong to the Lord who saved us, so to your relationship as a couple is meant for something larger than yourselves. A global mission. A co-mission meant to be lived out together! Have you ever thought about it that way before?

Have you ever thought that your relationship itself has a purpose for existence? You may not know the details of your life's calling yet. You may not even know what two years down the road looks like yet. Heck, you might not even know if you're meant to be with the person you're together with right now. But that doesn't mean you don't have a purpose and a calling to live out.

Whether you've been together for years now and you just gave your lives to Christ, or you just met last month and you really hit it off, it's time to start pursuing your purpose together. It's time to start feeling out what your calling might be. <u>And first and foremost, in order to discover those things, it's time to start carrying out your co-mission</u>!

How might your relationship look, feel, or even be different if you imbued it with Christ's purposes? Instead of just your daily priorities? How much deeper would your relationship together be if you instilled God's purposes into it, instead of these day-to-day pursuits? Would you get plugged in with other believers at your local church every weekend? Would you start taking time out of your busy day and start praying for those around you? Would you finally pick up that Bible, buy a new one you actually understand the language of, or just download the Bible app itself and let his healing words wash over you? Would you sign up for a small group and do life together with people who know your deepest joys and hurts and know when you're not there? Would you take up a cause worth fighting for and serve others, fighting the good fight? What would your life look like if you pursued his purposes together? How much better would your life be if you discovered his calling for it? How radically transformed would the relationship you're in together right now be if you did all these things together, hand in hand, carrying out the mission? The great co-mission!

I believe living out our co-mission was the single most unifying aspect of our relationship. We served together every single week, fighting against the principalities and unseen forces of hell. Which helped unite our hearts, it helped reconcile us quicker, forgive each other deeper and ultimately focus our fight on the enemy instead of each other. Living in community with others, and hearing their hurts and wounds kept us busy praying for others instead of finding faults in each other. Starting our individual days with Jesus in his word first helped us be more Christ-like to each other, more loving and compassionate. Worshipping Jesus every weekend at our worship service brought us back to the place of surrendering our relationship to him, instead of trying to control every inch and detail not going as planned. Living this calling out transformed our relationship in ways we can't even comprehend. And no matter what our lives looked like before we got to this point, purposefully living out his co-mission equipped us with everything we needed to move forward.

It doesn't matter how you got here. Or what your life looks like. If you have given it to God, received his grace through Jesus Christ and are ready to follow his Spirit's leading in your life, it's time to pick up your cross and get moving. And as you live out this co-mission, day after day, you'll discover layer after layer of worldly thinking, sinful desires and philosophies and priorities meant to distract you begin to peel right off. And more and more of the real you will begin to emerge. The you without this created world's tarnish. The you before this world ever began. That holy calling and eternal purpose imbued into the very core of who you are will begin to surface as you become more and more like Christ. A journey, an adventure meant to be done together in fellowship. A mission meant to be lived out together with your life-saving counterpart. "For it is not good for man to be alone." Are you pursuing the co-mission?

Individual Devotion (15 Minutes)

1) How much closer have you gotten to Christ looking back from last

   year?

   a) Did you ever picture being as close to God as you are now? Or

      perhaps you thought you'd be closer than you are now?

2) How might your relationship look, feel, or even be different if you

   imbued it with Christ's purposes, instead of your daily priorities?

3) How might your relationship improve if you did begin to live out the

   commission Christ has given each of us?

Couples Devotional (15 Minutes)

1) Does the great commission from Jesus to us his followers have any

   implications in the way we're currently living?

   a) How so?

2) Have you ever thought of our relationship being meant for something

   larger than just the two of us and our happiness?

3) How might your relationship grow stronger together if you started

   attending a worship service every weekend, or getting plugged in and

   start serving, or reading scripture daily, or joining a small group and started taking on some responsibility for something in your local church body?

4) How can we begin to fulfill our calling collectively as Christ followers and start living out the great commission?

   a) What are some of the things stopping or hindering us?

Application
Start praying over the areas of your life lacking in purpose and mission, and find a way to get plugged in further in your home church. Send an email, make a call, or chat with a leader or pastor next opportunity and get plugged into the mission of the church. Stop making excuses.

Chapter 17

Puppy Dogs and Ice Cream

[24] Then Jesus said to his disciples, "If any of you wants to be my follower, you must give up your own way, take up your cross, and follow me. [25] If you try to hang on to your life, you will lose it. But if you give up your life for my sake, you will save it. [26] And what do you benefit if you gain the whole world but lose your own soul? Is anything worth more than your soul? - Matthew 16:24-26
Also read Luke 9:21-27 / 1 Peter 1:6-7 / Proverbs 27:17

I know we've been using a lot of impacted words in this section. Words like calling and purpose and mission. And I know these last couple of chapters haven't been too practical either. I mean how could we practically go into the next steps for the plethora of different people this book might reach when it comes to their specific purpose or calling? But there are *some* practical things we can take away when it comes to purpose and your relationship. And believe me, if there is a constant, continual, never ending purpose for your relationship together from this point on into marriage and even until we reach eternity, it is this... Well, read the following.

The Christian walk with God is not an easy one. And the troubling thing to say is that no matter what stage of life you're in, life only gets harder and more hectic and more stressful to say the least! It always cracks me up to see graduating high school students or college students think that life will only get better now that they're going into the *real world*. It cracks me up because they think better doesn't equate to harder.

And this is especially true when we start following Jesus in the real world. Things like fleeing from temptation and denying ourselves are no light matter when we're on our own. Which is why your relationship shouldn't be a light matter to you either. It should have purpose. A real purpose. And even if your purpose for getting together (no matter what that entailed) was a fickle one, God's purpose for your relationship will have its way, if you let it. And it won't always feel like puppy dogs and ice cream.

Plainly put, one of God's main purposes in your relationship will be to drive the *hell* and *sin* out of you. Think about this, one of the main analogies and invitations Jesus used/uses to invite people to be a Christ follower was/is to pick up an instrument of the most immense torture and death each and every day and follow him. Now on top of you picking up your instrument of radical suffering, throw in your loved one who is also picking up their torture tool daily into the mix, and you begin to see that being together won't always be bliss. I think the term die daily should paint that portrait vividly for us.

Not a literal death, sure, but an even more painful experience if you ask me. The killing of your pride. And killing your lust. Killing your greed and coveting. Killing your secret life; you know, all the things you do at night or when you're alone and never plan on telling anyone. Killing your legalism, and your rigid religiousness. Killing your comfort-zone. killing your un-forgiveness. Killing your mental framework for how you think your life should go. Killing all that separates your likeness with Christ. Dying Daily.

One literal death would not even come close to transforming who we are now into the person Christ desires us to be for all eternity. Maybe that's why he incites us to die daily, it's a process. A refining process like Peter puts it, burning away all the impurities, the temporal. Even when our robust character in Christ is formed and the pressures and trials of this world have shaped us to be more like him; the Bible goes on to mention the sharpening of our character with iron sharpening iron. Thanks for the daunting imagery God, sounds super fun!

Now take all those imageries, like dying on a cross through immense suffering and excruciating asphyxiation from blood filling up your lungs. Plus the intolerable, face melting heat slowly burning away all that life has imbued in you as your plunged in molten metal like *Terminator* to burn away those deep seeded impurities. And don't forget iron striking iron in a continuous and recurring process. And we begin to see the game plan for kingdom character-development. Did we really think dating and being in a relationship with someone undergoing the exact same thing was *not* going to suck sometimes?

I don't know the purpose behind why you ended up with each other. Maybe you were tired of being lonely after all the destruction and ruin a former relationship entailed and you have hope God can bring light into those darkest regions of hurt. Or perhaps you didn't think that one night stand was going to turn into something more. Either way, no matter what purpose, or lack thereof, I can tell you this. <u>God's purpose for it, if you let him, will be to drive the hell, the sin and the worldly characteristics you've adopted straight out of your life</u>.

That sweet incredible person you thought could do no wrong will have you thinking *what* the *hell?* More often than not! That person who makes you laugh and smile and giggle with all those tickles will be the same person at times that makes you wonder how the *hell* did we end up arguing about this again? Yes, your lovey-wovey-dovey-snuggle-bear will get your frustration levels burning at *hell-fire* quicker than you can say Jesus loves me this I know. And it's in those moments that God wants to empower you to face the *sin* in you and overcome the *hell* in you.

The honeymoon phase ended for mine and Peyton's dating relationship right around month six. By then familiarity had bred transparency and idiosyncrasies broke our rose colored glasses. The gloves were off. We were fighting more than Mike Tyson in the nineties! And what do you expect? Being a pastor or a passionate Christ follower doesn't change anything. It makes it harder! She's imperfect, I'm really imperfect, and we're in a relationship intentionally centered around Jesus and what the Bible commands. All the while serving twice a week in ministry pursuing our purpose together. Of course all hell would break loose and come against us! As it will for you too. Of course the sinful nature in us would flare up like hell fire! And let me flat-out say it, of course things will not always be ok! And believe it or not, that's ok.

It's ok to not always be ok. It's ok to argue, fight, or just *strongly disagree* as you phrase it to all of your Christian brothers and sisters. God has a purpose for it, a purpose for you, and a purpose for this relationship. These moments of trials are opportunities for you to lean on your Heavenly Father. All of those moments of anxiety and fear allow you to depend on God and more fully trust in our Father. Every single gut-wrenching, knock-down, drag-out fight is another chance to surrender your so called *control* to God and let him be the sustainer and leader of your relationship and joy. <u>Every blow up is another opportunity to make up and reconcile through Christ-like forgiveness and love</u>. All the deep seeded insecurities a deep relationship digs up is another opportunity to let Jesus cultivate the soil of your heart, and allow his love to better grow throughout every facet of your life.

You might not know your purpose in life yet. And your relationship may not have begun with the best intentions or purposes in mind. You might not even make it as a couple. But keep putting Jesus first in it every day. And he will breathe God-inspired purpose into it. He will bring a purpose to all of the ugliness it's experienced. <u>He will bring purpose and new life to it if you pick up your crosses together and die daily</u>. God wants to drive the hell and sin and worldliness out of you to prepare you for an eternity with him in heaven.

Individual Devotion (15 Minutes)

1) Have you ever thought about the idea that God will use your significant other to drive the *hell* out of you and give you the opportunity to become more like Christ?

2) What situations might God be allowing in your life right now to give you the opportunity to be refined?

3) How often do I give in and respond like hell when circumstances don't go my way or my sin nature flares up.

Couples Devotional (15 Minutes)

1) What brought us together? Good intentions, or not so good?

   a) How can Christ begin to be glorified no matter how our relationship started?

2) When we first got together, did you ever picture fighting as much as you do now? Or if it's more recent, can you picture fighting as much as normal couples fight?

3) Can you think of any moments where we had the opportunity to turn to God, ask him to empower us, and overcome how our sinful nature wanted to respond?

   a) How did we respond?

4) How often do we respond negatively when circumstances don't go

   our way and hell breaks loose?

   a) How can we let Christ correct and refine us in those moments?

5) Honestly reflecting, is God the sustainer of our relationship? Or do we

   keep it going in our own strength?

   a) Is it our job to constantly fix what's wrong with each other?

6) Have you ever thought of every blow up as an opportunity to make

   up and reconcile through Christ-like forgiveness and love?

Application

Talking about fighting and blow-ups, talk with each other, and with a lot of grace list out the different things that cause blow-ups between you. This isn't a list to condemn one another. But an honest assessment of areas in your life you need to surrender to Christ. In your personal time, give these to Christ and ask him to help you and begin to change your heart more like his.

Chapter 18

Old Testament - New Testament

[20] After supper he took another cup of wine and said, "This cup is the new covenant between God and his people—an agreement confirmed with my blood, which is poured out as a sacrifice for you. - Luke 22:20
Also read Jeremiah 31:31-34 / Hebrews 8:6 / Romans 7:6

Can I just say it, dating sucks! Well at least dating in a Christ honoring way does. Ok, let me clarify, compared to how indescribable being married to Peyton is, dating sucked. And I'm willing to go out on a limb and say a lot of now-married Christians who did it God's way and didn't sleep together will tell you the same. Compared to marriage, dating sucks!

Looking back it was nothing but rules and regulations we had to bind ourselves with just to keep us away from the no-no-cha-cha dance. There was no freedom. It was constricting how restricting our precautions had to be just to make it to the altar in one piece. It was a time so entrenched with rules and regulations Peyton and I nicknamed it being in the Old-Testament.

Sure we had the most fun we could on dates, but we realized the season we were in was not the most exciting, or fun and even sucked at times. We recognized there will be a season that sets us free from the binds our relationship was currently in. It took time to fully recognize the rules and regulations defining our relationship now were necessary to set us up for the bliss and joy of the coming season, marriage. We knew full well this season would not last; God was about to do something new and outstanding in our lives at just the perfect time when we finally get up there and say our *I-do's*.

There was something powerful to this perspective. The perspective that this wouldn't last forever. Knowing God had a purpose for the season we were in now. Believing God's word that with Christ, our best days are always in front of us. It gave us strength when we were feeling weak and wanted to give in. It gave us hope when trying to traverse all the financial necessities and responsibilities preparing for marriage can bring. This perspective gave us life when we were worn and weary, wondering if things would ever change. <u>And most importantly of all, it brought purpose to waiting and keeping sex in the confines of marriage.</u>

I'm sure comparing what we felt (trying *not* to do what every hormone in our body was screaming out to do, mate), to the plight of trying to observe all six-hundred and thirteen Old Testament Levitical Laws is pretty audacious of us, but we couldn't help to see the correlations. Think about it, your current relationship is not meant to be like this forever. Just as God knew full well a better covenant and relationship with his people was coming. He loved his people enough to hand them a covenant that would get them there in one piece. And just like the fierce objectivity of the law exposes the depth of our sinfulness and the necessity for a savior; so to keeping his commands in dating and fleeing from sexual immorality teaches us reliance on Christ and how much we truly need him as the sustainer of our relationship. And just as there was a *perfect time* for when things had to pass in preparation for the messiah and New Covenant, so to our lives require certain markers and other obligations fulfilled (financially, responsibility, maturity) to be prepared for this new time. And the scariest comparison of all in my mind; is just as God's people were able to miss what God was doing right in front of them by hardening their hearts and perverting their relationship with him. Completely missing the New Covenant and who Jesus was/is. This is just like what we as God's people today can get stuck doing in our current season, never reaching the New Covenant season of our relationship by giving into *our way* of doing things. Instead of obeying his way.

Like the Pharisees who murdered Jesus and thought they were doing things *God's way*, we too can pervert our hearts and kill what Jesus is doing in our lives by giving into our sinful desires and excusing them through empty rituals like showing up church and Bible studies. God calls that kind of worship lip-service if your heart is obeying a different master. Sacrificing our Sunday morning for God doesn't cover up our lack of obedience on Friday night.

So let's open up our eyes! Looking forward to the coming season like the angels and prophets who were looking ahead. Prepare yourself for the coming season; get that career started, finish your last few credits, maybe start saving more aggressively, finally put your budget together, and get some premarital counseling. Prepare the way like John the Baptist did. Obey the commandments of the current season you're in, so your heart can be fully reliant on God and won't miss the indescribable-ness of what is coming next!

Let God's promises bring purpose to this season you're in as a couple! Let his promises bring purpose to your obedience. Do it God's way and let him pave the way for your relationship, getting you through those rocky times ahead. This season will end! Peyton and I were there, we know what it's like to fight the good fight, to flee from temptation and live in his purpose for us. We were right there with you and we can tell you truthfully these current hardships will not last forever. But he will, and his word will never fail you!

Peyton and I struggled with this like every human does. We would push the limits and get pissed at ourselves for doing so. Looking back it was kind of ridiculous to think human nature wouldn't push us to the limits of temptation considering the fact that even though we are Christ followers, we are still humans in the flesh. We would push the boundaries, and become immensely convicted! It got to the point where we had to add even more rules and regulations on top of all the other rules and regulations. I'm pretty sure by the end of our engagement we only allowed ourselves to hang out at her house. Never in her room for more than a short span of time. Eleven-thirty was pretty much the time to head home considering the fact that nothing *good* goes on after midnight for a Christ follower. No making-out. No spooning. I mean the list goes on and on. By the end of the engagement our relationship was drenched in these parameters. About three hundred and sixteen of them.

We would push the limits, add a boundary. We'd test the boundaries, add a regulation. Whatever it took to help us keep our eyes focused on the new season and relationship ahead, we did. We had to put these rules in place to keep our hopes focused on the freedom of marriage ahead. The New Testament like freedom.

And the funniest part of all, by the time we did reach the end of our engagement, these parameters didn't even matter. We were so close to being married I didn't need to give into current desires. We were almost there. I can say with all transparency, a month before the wedding I didn't have those desires at all anymore. Because I arrived, I was at the finish line. The old was leaving and the new was here. We made it.

And truth be told, you're almost there too. In hindsight, a couple months, a year, or five years is like the blinking of an eye as you get older.

Enjoy the season you're in. Let his promises bring purity to your relationship. You're not not having sex, because sex is bad or something like that. You're not *not* having sex because you know and believe when you do it God's way he'll pave the way for your relationship through heaven and hell. Trust in his promises. He has a purpose for your season. We'll talk more about purpose and sex in the following chapter.

Individual Devotional (15 Minutes)

1) Have you ever thought about the boundaries of dating today as the building blocks of trust and faith in your marriage?

2) What do you think are some of the lessons Christ wants you to learn in your current season?

3) Looking at the practical issues, are you financially, vocationally, and responsibly ready enough for God to bring you towards marriage sooner than later?

Couples Devotional (15 Minutes)

1) What are some of the current boundaries you have put in place during this time of dating to do it *God's way*?

   a) What might the lack of healthy boundaries say about our trust in Christ?

2) What do you think are some of the lessons Christ wants us to learn in our current season?

3) How can we start to let Christ sustain the boundaries his word instills in this season we're in, instead of trying to do it in our own strength?

4) Honestly reflecting and looking at our relationship, have we been

doing it our way, allowing sin to have its way, or have we been doing

it his way?

Application
Take an honest assessment of your relationship. What are some of the practical boundaries you need to put in place today to start doing it God's way and let his strength get you to the altar in one piece.

Chapter 19

Sex is Powerful

[1] Finally, dear brothers and sisters, we urge you in the name of the Lord Jesus to live in a way that pleases God, as we have taught you. You live this way already, and we encourage you to do so even more. [2] For you remember what we taught you by the authority of the Lord Jesus.

[3] God's will is for you to be holy, so stay away from all sexual sin. [4] Then each of you will control his own body and live in holiness and honor, [5] not in lustful passion like the pagans who do not know God and his ways. [6] Never harm or cheat a fellow believer in this matter by violating his wife, for the Lord avenges all such sins, as we have solemnly warned you before. [7] God has called us to live holy lives, not impure lives. [8] Therefore, anyone who refuses to live by these rules is not disobeying human teaching but is rejecting God, who gives his Holy Spirit to you.
– 1 Thessalonians 4:1-8
Also read all of Romans 6 / 1 Corinthians 6:9-20

Nothing is new under the sun Solomon said about three thousand years ago. And it still rings true today. Of course our technology has advanced and improved, but technology is a tool for many different things, and we've been improving our tools and technology since the wheel. And since nothing is truly new under the sun, don't be surprised and think this is a new commandment just recently made up and put in the Bible; **no sex** outside of marriage. Crazy right? And I know everyone else is literally *doing it*, but how can we as Jesus followers continue in sin if we have died to sin and live in God's power? That same type of power that rose Jesus from the grave. But as Solomon said, nothing is new under the sun, and living in a society that promotes sex isn't new either. Living in a sexually over-charged society isn't something this world has never faced before because this generation is *extra sinful* or something. As a matter of fact, sexual immorality is not at an all-time high, since it's never really been at an all-time low in human existence.

It's been so prevalent throughout the human condition that the apostle Paul has to refer to it and teach against it in almost every single letter to the churches found in the New Testament. "For no other sin so clearly affects the *body*," he wrote to the Corinthians, "For sexual immorality is a sin against your own *body*. Or don't you know that your *body* is the temple of the Holy Spirit who lives in you and was given to you by God?" How is it that we've somehow missed this part of Jesus' words to us? Really, why do we ignore this part of the Bible in our lives as a whole?

To me, it seems like every generation has been cool with Jesus' commandments to love God and to love others as we love ourselves and go around the world preaching free love and grace and hope. It's hard not to be cool with those things. Yet when his word begins to affect your booty call routine, that's when we get *blurred lines*? As the scripture begins to point its edge at your friendship-with-benefits, that's when things get too personal? When the word of God directly opposes what you and your girlfriend won't stop doing, that's when things get too radical for us to follow and believe?

But look back to what Paul said, "No other sin so clearly affects the body, the temple of the Holy Spirit." There is purpose behind these commandments, and all of God's word demands we flee from it. It's not that God's a prude, *He actually invented sex*, no matter what Trey Songz claims. God invented sex for us to enjoy. But he invented its explosive ecstasies to be enjoyed within the safe confines of marriage.

Sex is powerful, which is the purpose we as followers of Jesus flee from *Netflix and chilling*. Sex was designed to take two completely separate people and biochemically unify them with one another for life. Go research the chemistry of what happens in the brain during intercourse. Even before this research, for centuries people weren't considered man and wife until they consummated their marriage with sex, not just a ceremony, because it changes everything. Sex is so powerful, it takes the two individual's DNA strands and infuses them together, becoming one, and creating a child, a new life. Probably just one of the reasons Jesus testified to the Garden of Eden account when he quotes *the two become one*.

Now take this over-simplistic overview, along with the infinite amount of other things researchers are still discovering about sex, multiply it by all the things God says about it, and you have yourself a power that can destroy your body, the temple of the Holy Spirit like no other sin can! And not just your personal *body*, but the *church body* you collectively belong to. Maybe that's why Paul tells us the Corinthians in 1

Corinthians 5 to teach that sexually immoral man sleeping with his father's wife, *that's not ok dude*. Don't you know that if even one person is allowed to go on sinning soon all will think it's cool?

The word *body* there that Paul uses is the Greek word *Soma*. And Soma has some other meanings layered in it other than just your human body. Soma is a Greek word used a hundred and forty-six times in the New Testament also referring to the *body of believers*, the church. Which gives a complete imagery when the apostle Peter also refers to us individual believers as "Living stones that God is building into his spiritual temple," in 1 Peter 2:5. Are you starting to see the connection?

What's one of the purposes we don't have sex before marriage? Because it's powerful! <u>No other sin so clearly affects your personal body, and the church body you're connected to.</u> Your *Hulu and Hanging* destroys what the Holy Spirit wants to do in you. Your *Amazon Prime and playing* kills the Holy Spirit's work. *A sex-life before marriage kills all the work of new life the Holy Spirit wants to do in you and through you*. All the work God wants to do in your life, choosing to sin quenches the spirit as we read in 1 Thessalonians 5:19.

The word quench here paints the picture of extinguishing a fire. Choosing to sin puts out the spirit's work in you like a fire gets put out and extinguished. Maybe that's why John the Baptist prophesied Jesus would baptize us with *spirit and fire*: only to have the Father fulfill it a few years later in that upper room on the Jewish holiday of Pentecost when the Holy Spirit was first given, descending like *tongues of fire*. No other sin will *quench* and destroy what the spirit wants to do in you like sex outside of marriage.

Sex is powerful; it takes two people and makes them one. <u>Sex was designed to be powerful on purpose for a purpose; marriage</u>. Outside of marriage, not only will it crumble your personal relationship with Christ, but it will also hinder, quench and destroy what the Holy Spirit wants to do through you in the church body you're apart of too. And Paul didn't need just spiritual insight to prove this fact. As a church planter, raising up bodies of believers all over the Mediterranean, I bet he's seen firsthand how quickly and clearly sexual immorality destroys the bodies he's tried to raise up in faith. I bet after seeing a couple meltdowns, Paul knew exactly what to say to this Corinthian church in regards to the guy sleeping with his dad's wife. Get him out! Get him out before everyone thinks sexual immorality ain't that harmful. Get him out or everyone else, every other living stone making up that body and spiritual temple will be affected. He needed some time to reflect on his decisions before they welcomed him back in. And as a pastor today I don't need spiritual revelations to see how many churches split, crumble and die because their pastor, or elder, or deacon screwed around. And truth be told, neither do you.

What's the purpose behind not having sex outside of marriage? What are *a few* good reasons we as Christ followers should avoid the no pants dance, even with the person you might end up marrying? What is one single purpose, not just moral priority, I should put my pants back on and sprint to my car if my significant other begins to take their pants off? Because sex is powerful. And it will destroy the spirit's work in us and through us in our local body we're a part of.

Last thought. It's kind of scary to me when I think back to Jesus' words he tells the disciples, "The gates of hell shall not prevail against this church." Yet a few books later, his word also tell us, sexual immorality can affect us in a unique way that no other sin can, individually and collectively as a church. It's kind of scary to think sexual immorality can hurt us in a way that hell itself can't even do. What does that tell you about how powerful a little sex is?

Individual Devotional (15 Minutes)

1) What do you think are some ways society has influenced your view of sex?

2) Without getting judgmental, who are some Christ followers you know that allowed sex in their dating and how has that visibly affected their faith, relationship with Christ or with other believers or within the ministry they're apart of?

3) How might sexual immorality be hindering the Holy Spirit's work in your life today?

4) Take an honest assessment, are you feeding the fire of the Holy Spirit through obedience and faith, or are sinful choices extinguishing his leading and presence in your life?

Couples Devotional (15 Minutes)

1) What does our culture say about sex and how is that different from scripture?

   a) What does the Christian culture you're in say about sex and how might that be different than what scripture says about sex?

2) How have you seen sexual immorality destroy someone's life, or destroy their church?

3) How might allowing sexual immorality and sleeping together now

   outside of marriage impact what God wants to do through you?

Application

Order, or pick up a copy of the book, *The Five Love Languages*. As this devotional comes to a close, take the love language test and discuss your results. Write down the different ways you can specifically demonstrate and better receive each other's love and affection without needing to involve sex into the equation. Then go through that book together after this one.

Closing Chapter

[10] For we are God's masterpiece. He has created us anew in Christ Jesus, so we can do the good things he planned for us long ago. - Ephesians 2:10

As we wrap up, I wish I could tell you so much more! I wish Peyton and I could sit down over coffee with you and encourage you. We'd assure you that God is able to do exceedingly and abundantly above all you could ever expect in and through your relationship if you let him. Don't give up, don't give in! Fight the good fight, run this race with endurance!

As a married couple, we are coming up on our one year wedding anniversary in May and it feels like just yesterday we were where you are today. Unofficial and going on dates every week. Or a few months into our *Facebook official* relationship, enjoying the bliss of the honeymoon phase. Even the hardship of trying to make it through our first set of real rough patches seems like not that long ago. Looking back it kind of all blurs together into one; all those experiences and memories blending into one, just like a plethora of paint comes together and merges into one painting.

The good and the bad, the dark times and the light-hearted times all culminating into one beautiful portrait, our dating journey. But that masterpiece is just one of many to be painted in this gallery of life. As we navigate all the mountains and valleys marriage provides, I just want to encourage you as this devotional comes to a close; do it his way. It's worth it.

As we navigate our first year in marriage, I truly believe we are reaping a harvest of blessing today because of the seeds we sowed yesterday. Our relationship, our finances, our vocations, our ministries, all aligned and full of joy. And that's not due to our aptitude of being an overly-successful couple, but simply because we've aligned them all to what his word says. We had faith that God brought us together for a reason, and faith equals obedience in action. And obey we did, no matter how painful it got and still gets.

I hope you found these chapters clarifying and encouraging when it comes to building your relationship on his foundation and his frame for painting within. In that portrait I can see the highlights of bright colors when obedience felt like blessing. I see accents of dark when it felt more like dying. And even though our lives and stories are completely different, God will use these similar shades and hues in your relationship as well. And no matter how brilliant or how bleak the colors you expect the canvas of your relationship to be defined with, he will work it all together. And he'll work it together for good, into a masterpiece.

And you are his masterpiece. Individually and collectively, he will create newness through Christ Jesus in your life. It may be a turning point in your relationship where your heart screams yes, and you choose to die to your sin, commit all to him, and let his blood cleanse you as new. It may be from before you ever make it official, laying the very first bricks of your relationship foundation his way through obedience. Whatever, however, he wants to blend these random experiences, moments and memories of your life together in one culminating masterpiece that gives glory to our Father. A masterpiece planned long ago and culminated by his perfect craftsmanship. A plan for your relationship and life involving good things, not bad. He's a good, good Father. Trust him with your relationship, trust him with your money, trust him with your time. Surrender your life to him, surrender your relationship to him and watch what miracles he can perform on the canvas of your existence when you give him control of the brush.

Made in the USA
Lexington, KY
12 January 2017